THE BEDFORD SERIES IN HISTORY AND CULTURE

Radical Reconstruction

A Brief History with Documents

Radical Reconstruction

A Brief History with Documents

K. Stephen Prince

University of South Florida

Bedford/St. Martin's
A Macmillan Education Imprint

Boston • New York

For Bedford/St. Martin's

Vice President, Editorial, Macmillan Higher Education Humanities: Edwin Hill
Publisher for History: Michael Rosenberg
Senior Executive Editor for History: William J. Lombardo
Director of Development for History: Jane Knetzger
Developmental Editor: Heidi Hood
Production Editor: Lidia MacDonald-Carr
Production Supervisors: Victoria Anzalone and Carolyn Quimby
Executive Marketing Manager: Sandra McGuire
Project Management: Books By Design, Inc.
Cartography: Mapping Specialists, Ltd.
Director of Rights and Permissions: Hilary Newman
Senior Art Director: Anna Palchik
Text Design: Claire Seng-Niemoeller
Cover Design: William Boardman
Composition: Achorn International, Inc.
Printing and Binding: RR Donnelley and Sons

Manufactured in the United States of America.

0   9   8   7   6   5
f   e   d   c   b   a

For information, write: Bedford/St. Martin's, 75 Arlington Street, Boston, MA 02116
(617-399-4000)

ISBN 978-1-4576-6934-7

Acknowledgments

Foreword

The Bedford Series in History and Culture is designed so that readers can study the past as historians do.

The historian's first task is finding the evidence. Documents, letters, memoirs, interviews, pictures, movies, novels, or poems can provide facts and clues. Then the historian questions and compares the sources. There is more to do than in a courtroom, for hearsay evidence is welcome, and the historian is usually looking for answers beyond act and motive. Different views of an event may be as important as a single verdict. How a story is told may yield as much information as what it says.

Along the way the historian seeks help from other historians and perhaps from specialists in other disciplines. Finally, it is time to write, to decide on an interpretation and how to arrange the evidence for readers.

Each book in this series contains an important historical document or group of documents, each document a witness from the past and open to interpretation in different ways. The documents are combined with some element of historical narrative — an introduction or a biographical essay, for example — that provides students with an analysis of the primary source material and important background information about the world in which it was produced.

Each book in the series focuses on a specific topic within a specific historical period. Each provides a basis for lively thought and discussion about several aspects of the topic and the historian's role. Each is short enough (and inexpensive enough) to be a reasonable one-week assignment in a college course. Whether as classroom or personal reading, each book in the series provides firsthand experience of the challenge — and fun — of discovering, recreating, and interpreting the past.

Lynn Hunt
David W. Blight
Bonnie G. Smith

Preface

Few periods in U.S. history were as politically transformative, as violently contested, as rife with promise and peril as Reconstruction. In the aftermath of the Civil War, political leaders faced a variety of momentous questions concerning the place of the southern states in the postwar nation, the status of formerly enslaved African Americans, and the powers and limitations of the federal government. In spite of its historical significance, many students struggle to understand Reconstruction. The period's chronological sweep and geographic diversity can be confusing; when faced with an array of unfamiliar names, dates, places, and acts, it is easy to miss the larger significance of the era. This volume seeks to clarify both the specifics and the larger historical context, allowing students to access the drama, the struggle, and the power of Reconstruction through a short, clearly written introduction and a selection of representative documents.

While this volume is designed to offer an overview of the entire Reconstruction period, it focuses most closely on the political history of the early postwar years, an era frequently referred to as "Radical Reconstruction." This term, it should be noted, refers simultaneously to a moment in time (roughly 1866 to 1868), a body of legislation (including the Fourteenth Amendment and the Reconstruction Act of 1867), and a group of historical actors (the Radical Republicans). Throughout the volume, I have worked to maintain this triple focus.

Part One, the Introduction, opens with a discussion of the Radical Republicans, a group of senators and representatives who gained prominence in the early postwar years. Having described the Radicals' political worldview, the Introduction shows that Reconstruction actually grew out of a complex negotiation among a variety of groups with distinct, often conflicting, agendas. Along with the Radicals, therefore, the Introduction examines the words and deeds of President Andrew Johnson, moderate and conservative Republicans in Congress, white southerners, and former slaves. Although the Introduction offers the greatest detail on the period from 1866 to 1868, it also discusses the administration of Ulysses S. Grant, the violence of southern Redemption, and the legacies of Radical Reconstruction.

The documents that make up Part Two are designed to shed light on the evolution of federal policy in the aftermath of the Civil War. Included are most of the period's major legislative enactments, all three of the "Reconstruction Amendments" to the U.S. Constitution, and a selection of speeches and writings by influential Radicals such as Thaddeus Stevens and Charles Sumner. A variety of other documents—including the writings of moderate and conservative Republicans, President Andrew Johnson's speeches and veto messages, and popular commentary on Reconstruction—are included to provide background and context. Throughout, special attention is paid to the words and deeds of African Americans in the North and the South.

For the most part, the documents in Part Two are organized chronologically, although I have occasionally deviated from this structure in order to aid student comprehension. The selections in Chapter 1 concern wartime debates over Reconstruction and Andrew Johnson's lenient southern policy. Chapter 2 introduces congressional Reconstruction and the quest to protect African American civil rights, culminating in the Fourteenth Amendment. The documents in Chapter 3 take readers through the election of 1866, the Reconstruction Act of 1867, and the advent of black suffrage. Chapter 4 describes the impeachment of Andrew Johnson and the election of Ulysses S. Grant. In Chapter 5, the selections detail the violence of Redemption and the nation's retreat from the racial egalitarianism of Reconstruction.

A century and a half after the events they describe, these documents retain their poignancy and immediacy. Even so, a number of student aids have been provided to facilitate classroom use. An analytical headnote, designed to provide historical context and to aid in comprehension, accompanies each document. Where further explanation of a specific term or reference is needed, explanatory footnotes have been provided. The appendix to this volume also includes a brief chronology of Reconstruction, a selection of questions designed to foster classroom discussion and spur student analysis, and a bibliography with some suggestions for further study.

ACKNOWLEDGMENTS

First of all, a thank-you to David Blight, without whom this volume would not exist—at least, not with me as the author. The helpful responses prepared by reviewers Jessica Cannon of the University of Central Missouri; Brian Craig Miller of Emporia State University; Alan Downs of Georgia Southern University; Jennifer Gross of Jacksonville State University; Kate Masur of Northwestern University; and Joan Waugh of the University of California, Los Angeles, have made this a much stronger book.

Special thanks are due to Kate Masur, who went above and beyond the call of duty, heroically line-editing the entire manuscript and offering extraordinarily detailed feedback. At Bedford/St. Martin's, Bill Lombardo was an early champion of the project, and generously handled my questions and my occasional lack of patience. Heidi Hood has been an ideal developmental editor, offering extraordinary feedback and clear guidance. Thanks are also due to Arrin Kaplan, Laura Kintz, Michael Rosenberg, Jane Knetzger, Sandi McGuire, Lidia MacDonald-Carr, and Nancy Benjamin.

My thanks go to the members of the history department at the University of South Florida for their support during this project. My parents, Ken and Jane Prince, and my sister, Allison Prince, aided in this volume even if they don't know it. My friends in Tampa kept me sane, happy, and well-fed while working on this book. Of course, the final shout-out must go to Julia Irwin, who read every word of the manuscript (several times) and dealt with my mutterings, grumblings, and musings throughout the whole process. Julia is the best colleague, spouse, and friend I could imagine.

Contents

Maps and Illustrations

PART ONE

Introduction: Who Were the Radical Republicans?

When Claude Bowers, an Indiana politician and amateur historian, set out to write the story of Reconstruction, he knew precisely who would play the bad guy. Bowers's 1929 work, *The Tragic Era: The Revolution after Lincoln*, is an unapologetic tale of good and evil. Bowers was a northerner, but he openly sided with the white South, arguing that after the Civil War, white southerners had been "put to the torture," suffering outrageous hardships and brutal oppression unmatched in United States history.[1] But who was the torturer? To anchor his tale, Bowers needed a treacherous and deceitful villain. After all, someone had to make "the tragic era" tragic. For this role, Bowers turned to Thaddeus Stevens, congressman from Pennsylvania and leader of the Radical Republicans, a group of senators and representatives who played an important part in setting Reconstruction policy in the first years after the Civil War. "Never have American public men in responsible positions, directing the destiny of the Nation, been so brutal, hypocritical, and corrupt," Bowers wrote of Stevens and the Radicals.[2] They were "unscrupulous gamblers" whose "personal ambition" and "party motives" nearly destroyed the South.[3] Bowers devoted an entire chapter to Stevens, describing him as a dictatorial and uncompromising party leader who saw in Reconstruction an opportunity to exact his revenge on "these hated men of the South."[4]

Historians have largely discredited Bowers's vision of a hellish Reconstruction led by scheming Radical Republicans.[5] And yet, depictions like his retain some purchase in American culture. Reconstruction

1

remains one of the most chronically misunderstood eras in U.S. history. Many Americans continue to disparage the period, imagining Reconstruction as a time of punitive legislation, federal overreach, and chronic corruption. At the heart of this misrepresentation stand the Radical Republicans. Much to the chagrin of their detractors, congressional Radical Republicans worked to expand the power of the federal government and set a course toward democracy and racial egalitarianism. Although the rise of Democratic regimes across the South undid much of the work of Republican Reconstruction by the mid-1870s, the period's legislative enactments forever reshaped the face of American society and governance. Far from vindictive and power-hungry monsters, congressional Radical Republicans espoused a truly inclusive political and social vision that placed them far ahead of the historical curve. In spite of their name, the Radical Republicans were not zealots. They offered a coherent vision of the nation's future, rooted in a clear-eyed understanding of the unprecedented challenges they faced in the aftermath of secession, Civil War, and emancipation.[6]

When the Civil War ended in April 1865, the United States faced a political crisis of startling magnitude. Somehow, the eleven states that had seceded to form the Confederacy had to be reintegrated into the United States. The exact procedure to be followed, however, was unclear. Should the process occur quickly, with few restrictions placed on the returning South? Or did four years of war and hundreds of thousands of dead American soldiers demand a more stringent readmission policy? Were the states of the South still *states*? Perhaps secession and war had dissolved statehood, reducing the South to the status of territories to be governed from Washington. And what of the South's former master class? Would high-ranking Confederate officials and officeholders be allowed to resume their position at the top of the South's political and economic hierarchy? If not, what sort of punishment should be imposed on the South's antebellum and wartime leadership?

The social revolution of emancipation, which freed four million African American slaves from bondage, raised an equally momentous set of questions. Most northerners agreed that the federal government bore some responsibility to protect the lives and liberties of the South's freedpeople. Beyond this, however, much was up for debate. How could the government best aid the transition to freedom? What specific steps were necessary to protect African Americans from exploitative labor practices and the potentially vindictive passions of their former masters? An additional set of questions related to the political status of the region's emancipated slaves. Should the South's freedpeople be considered citizens?

Should black men be given the right to vote? All of these questions (and more) confronted policymakers in the first years after the Civil War. Reconstruction proved to be one of the most violent and contentious periods in U.S. history precisely because so much was at stake. At issue in the immediate postwar period was nothing less than the character of the South and the future of the nation.

Congressional Radical Republicans recognized that the upheaval and devastation wrought by war offered a powerful opportunity to reform the South, and they did not intend to miss it. Led by Thaddeus Stevens in the House of Representatives and Charles Sumner of Massachusetts in the Senate, the Radical Republicans offered bold and uncompromising answers to the era's major political questions. From the outset, they denied that Reconstruction was a simple matter of restoration. The federal government, they argued, possessed both the right and the responsibility to eradicate the last vestiges of a debauched and corrupt slaveholding regime that had dragged the nation into a brutal civil war. More than this, they argued that emancipation constituted a solemn promise on the part of the nation and the Republican party. Radical Republicans considered themselves duty-bound to work toward the full integration of southern African Americans into the nation's political and civil life. They argued that race should have no bearing on citizenship and political participation, and they worked to build a color-blind democracy on the ruins of the South's slave oligarchy. Expressing a deep belief in the restorative power of American democracy, congressional Radical Republicans sought to turn the federal government into a force for equality and justice.[7]

While the Republican party enjoyed large majorities in both houses of Congress throughout the early years of Reconstruction, Radicals were always forced to compromise with more moderate elements within the party. Radical Reconstruction actually grew out of a series of compromises among the Republican party's Radical, moderate, and conservative wings. Indeed, staunch Radicals like Sumner and Stevens freely expressed their disappointment with the compromise measures that were able to secure majorities in both houses of Congress. The political realities of the era forced them to temper some of their more expansive dreams for the re-creation of the South. Even so, the legislative accomplishments of Radical Reconstruction remain landmarks in American history. The Radicals imagined a Reconstruction that would remake the South, protect the civil and political rights of the freedpeople, and ensure the cohesion and stability of the nation in the aftermath of the Civil War. More than this, they demanded that the nation embrace color-blind democracy and racial egalitarianism, arguing that anything less would be a betrayal of national ideals and the legacy of the Civil War. Americans have struggled to rise to their challenge ever since.

THE RADICALS' RECONSTRUCTION

On January 9, 1865, as the Civil War neared its conclusion, Ohio's Benjamin Wade held court on the floor of the Senate. Wade took the opportunity to describe his political creed, explaining, in effect, what made a Radical a Radical. "The radical men are the men of principle," Wade offered. "They are the men who feel what they contend for. They are not your slippery politicians who can jigger this way or that, or construe a thing any way to suit the present occasion. They are the men who go deeply down for principle, and having fixed their eyes upon a great principle connected with the liberty of mankind or the welfare of the people, are not to be detached by any of your haggling." For Wade, this guiding principle was a deep hatred of slavery. When he arrived in the Senate in the early 1850s, Wade recalled, he was one of a handful of committed abolitionists, a "miserable minority" too small to exercise any power in Washington. But Wade and the Radicals had persevered. Their steadfast commitment to principle had "regenerated" and "revolutionized" the nation. Slavery was on the road to extinction. Former bondsmen fought valiantly while wearing the blue of the Union army. The Confederacy was on its last legs. As the nation pivoted from war to Reconstruction, Wade promised that the Radicals would stand firm. Principle would be their guide, the nation's redemption their goal.[8]

   In his embrace of principle, Benjamin Wade was not alone. In the Senate, a small circle of self-conscious Radicals joined the combative Ohioan. The Senate's most visible and outspoken Radical was Charles Sumner. Joining the Senate in 1851, Sumner quickly made a name for himself as an eloquent and forceful opponent of slavery. After a particularly biting 1856 speech, South Carolina representative Preston Brooks attacked Sumner on the floor of the Senate, nearly beating him to death with a cane. Sumner was absent from the Senate for three years. Upon his return in 1859, however, he picked up where he left off. Throughout the Civil War and Reconstruction, Sumner was a consistent voice for racial equality and justice. His long-winded, scholarly speeches and his sizable ego did little to endear him to his colleagues in the Senate, but his unswerving support for African American rights made him the political conscience of the Republican party's Radical wing.[9]

Sumner's counterpart in the House of Representatives was Pennsylvania's Thaddeus Stevens. Like Sumner, Stevens was a passionate believer in African American civil and political rights. Colleagues admired his sincerity and feared his sarcastic wit. Stevens insisted that Congress had a duty to reform southern society in the aftermath of the Civil War; he had little patience for the hesitancy and hand wringing of more moderate Republicans. As the elder statesman of House Radicals—he was seventy-three at the end of the Civil War—Stevens remained a powerful voice in Congress until his death in 1868.[10] Other influential Radicals in the House of Representatives included George Julian of Indiana, James Ashley of Ohio, and George Boutwell of Massachusetts. Julian was a committed supporter of land redistribution in the South, while Ashley and Boutwell played leading roles in the impeachment of President Andrew Johnson.[11]

A coherent set of political principles united the Radical Republicans. Many of the Reconstruction-era Radicals got their start in the movement against slavery. With the notable exception of Stevens, most leading Radicals represented districts in New England and the upper Midwest where the antebellum reform impulse and abolitionism had established deep roots. These commitments shaped their approach to the Civil War and Reconstruction. During the war, congressional Radicals loudly called for the emancipation of the slaves. They voted to end slavery in the District of Columbia in 1862, they supported Abraham Lincoln's Emancipation Proclamation in 1863, and they were instrumental in the passage of the Thirteenth Amendment, banning slavery, in 1865.

Radicals held a deep commitment to racial equality and would continue to plead the cause of the South's African Americans after the war. As Massachusetts senator Henry Wilson put it, "I believe in equality among citizens—equality in the broadest and most comprehensive democratic sense."[12] To begin with, the Radicals insisted that the South's former slaves must be made citizens, with all the rights and privileges this status entailed. Certain rights—including access to federal and state courts, equitable treatment before the law, and the unfettered use of public space—should be guaranteed to the freedpeople. Radicals insisted that legal discrimination between the races was a grotesque perversion of the nation's founding creed, running contrary to the spirit of American institutions. Federal and state governments should be color-blind, with civil rights guaranteed to all regardless of race. The enactment and protection of this equality of basic rights was a cornerstone of Republican Reconstruction.

In contrast to their more moderate Republican colleagues, who vowed to secure the civil rights of the freedmen but initially declined to extend the vote to African Americans, Radicals argued that full political equality was both morally and strategically necessary. Most nineteenth-century political thinkers did not consider suffrage to be a right guaranteed by citizenship. They considered it, instead, a privilege that might reasonably be withheld from certain men (and all women). From the Radicals' perspective, however, this distinction was entirely nonsensical. They argued that the freedmen would remain at the mercy of their former masters until they were fully integrated into the body politic and armed with the vote. African American civil rights could not be secured without a corresponding increase in political rights. From the beginning, therefore, Radicals insisted that a comprehensive plan for Reconstruction must include suffrage for the South's freedmen.

A few Radicals went further than this, calling for the confiscation of land belonging to the wealthiest white southerners and its redistribution to the formerly enslaved. Advocates of confiscation, notably Stevens, Sumner, and Julian, argued that the interests of the freedpeople—and the nation—were in danger so long as large plantations continued to dominate the landscape of the South. Taking their cue from the North's system of free labor and small landownership, these Radicals sought to work a fundamental revolution in the economic structure of the South. While elite whites controlled huge tracts of prime land, the freedpeople would be forever beholden to the whims of their former masters. Freedpeople would be unable to advance beyond the degraded status of paid agricultural laborers. Confiscation would level the playing field, establishing the former slaves as a landed, self-sufficient class of small farmers. Needless to say, the call for the confiscation and redistribution of land was extraordinarily controversial, even among self-described Radicals. To many, confiscation seemed an unwarranted and indefensible violation of property rights. Supporters raised the land issue repeatedly during Reconstruction, but it never commanded widespread congressional support.

Underlying the Radicals' vision for the South was an expansive sense of the power of the federal government. During the Civil War, the federal government grew markedly, in terms of both its size and its responsibilities. Radicals supported this growth and after the war sought to use the federal government as an agent of change in the South. The Radicals uniformly insisted that the federal government had both the right and the responsibility to direct Reconstruction as it saw fit. The tradition of federalism, which emphasized the sovereign power of individual states, ran deep in American political culture. Radicals argued, however, that the Civil War had altered the balance of state and federal power. The eleven states of the Confederacy had seceded and made war on the United States. In so doing, they had surrendered their right to representation and to a say in the Reconstruction process. They were no longer sovereign states; they were vanquished enemies. For this reason, the federal government had the right to impose any conditions it deemed necessary—including African American citizenship and suffrage—before readmitting the seceded states to the Union. This point of view—often called the "grasp of war" doctrine—was at the heart of the Radicals' Reconstruction program.[13]

While they advocated concrete policies, there was always an element of idealism—even utopianism—to the Radical vision of Reconstruction. For the Radicals, the Confederacy's defeat marked a moment of unprecedented possibility. They believed that the South had long been a problem in American life. With its slave society and plantation economy, the region was an anomaly in a nation otherwise committed to free labor and small property ownership. In the immediate aftermath of the Civil War, however, the South's political, economic, and social structures suddenly appeared malleable. Confederate defeat had created a national opportunity. As Thaddeus Stevens put it, "The whole fabric of southern society *must* be changed, and never can it be done if this opportunity is lost" (Document 8).[14] Or, in Charles Sumner's words, "Congress must dare to be brave; it must dare to be just."[15] It was the dream of a South reborn that motivated Stevens, Sumner, and their allies throughout Reconstruction. The Radicals had one chance to re-create the South. The stakes were high, and time was short. Congress must act.

ALLIES AND ADVERSARIES

Of course, congressional Radical Republicans were not the sole arbiters of federal authority in the early Reconstruction period. More moderate and conservative voices within the Republican party held the Radicals' expansive ideological agenda in check. Although significant ideological differences separated Radicals from non-Radicals, matters of temperament were equally significant. Whereas Radicals such as Benjamin Wade loudly proclaimed their devotion to principle, moderate and conservative Republicans were more likely to concern themselves with practical matters: Was a piece of proposed legislation enforceable? Was it constitutional? How would it affect the political future of the Republican party (and by extension, the health of the larger Reconstruction endeavor)? Non-Radicals sincerely hoped to protect the rights of the freedpeople and to secure a safe transition from war to peace. However, they harbored significant doubts regarding the Radicals' expansive vision of federal authority.

Throughout Reconstruction, the moderate and conservative wings of the party exercised extraordinary influence in Congress. Because the Radicals did not have the votes to pass legislation on their own, their programs could only become law with the assent of non-Radicals. The most extreme parts of the Radical agenda, like land redistribution, were never able to secure this support and languished in Congress. Over time, however, a distinct shift occurred, as non-Radicals displayed an increasing willingness to embrace measures previously championed by their more idealistic colleagues. African American suffrage—which moved from a purely Radical position to Republican party orthodoxy in little more than two years—provides a case in point. Indeed, the course of Reconstruction legislation was defined, in large part, by the migration of moderate and conservative Republicans toward Radical positions. For this reason, attention to the words and deeds of influential non-Radicals (including Illinois senator Lyman Trumbull and Ohio senator John Sherman) is vital to a proper understanding of the political history of congressional Reconstruction. Simply put, there would have been no "Radical Reconstruction" without the support of congressional moderates and conservatives.

It is worth asking why moderate Republicans moved so far in a Radical direction in such a short period of time. A large part of the credit (or blame) for this political shift must be laid at the feet of President Andrew Johnson. When Johnson ascended to the presidency in April 1865, he set the South on a course to a speedy restoration. Pardoning the vast majority of former rebels, Johnson invited the states of the former Confederacy to hold elections and to send senators and representatives to Washington. Congressional Republicans—Radical and non-Radical alike—were disturbed by Johnson's haste and set about establishing their own Reconstruction policy. Johnson responded by adopting a strategy of antagonistic obstructionism, vetoing every piece of Reconstruction legislation that reached his desk. By late 1866, it was clear that congressional Republicans had an implacable enemy in the White House. All Reconstruction legislation would have to be passed over Johnson's veto, requiring a two-thirds majority in both houses of Congress. In such a context, Radicals and non-Radicals were forced to work together. The artificial cohesion that Johnson created helped to push congressional policy in a more Radical direction.[16]

Events outside Washington also influenced the course of Reconstruction. The actions of individual southerners, black and white, helped to shape congressional policy. For their part, southern African Americans quickly adapted to their new lives in freedom, displaying a keen political awareness and an unflinching loyalty to the federal government and the Republican party. In political meetings and state conventions held across the South, African Americans added their voice to the national conversation over Reconstruction (Document 27). From the moment of Confederate surrender, however, white southerners used all the resources at their disposal to subvert the Reconstruction process. Resorting to discriminatory legislation, economic coercion, and terrorist violence, the South's leadership class sought to deny the civil and political rights of African Americans and to ensure that black freedom bore as close a resemblance to slavery as possible.[17] Near constant southern racial discord forced congressional Republicans to take increasingly aggressive steps to protect the lives and rights of the freedpeople. This, in turn, heightened white southern resistance. The legislative agenda of Reconstruction grew out of this back-and-forth process. The increasing radicalization of federal policy was due, in large part, to the chronically unstable state of racial affairs in the South.

Although the Radicals entered the postwar period with a distinct vision and a clear plan for the South, the Reconstruction process itself necessarily altered those plans. The program that we know as "Radical Reconstruction" was actually the result of debate, contestation, and negotiation among a number of parties both inside and outside of Congress. The architects of Reconstruction policy responded to real historical circumstances and adjusted their plans accordingly. From this perspective, the obstinacy of Andrew Johnson and the resistance of the white South had as much to do with the course of Reconstruction as the political principles of Charles Sumner or Thaddeus Stevens.

WARTIME RECONSTRUCTION

To understand Reconstruction, one needs to look back to the Civil War. In a sense, Reconstruction actually began with the signing of the Emancipation Proclamation. Throughout the first year and a half of the Civil War, President Abraham Lincoln insisted that the national armies fought for Union, not emancipation. By mid-1862, however, as thousands of runaway slaves arrived in U.S. army camps every day, Lincoln began to consider the strategic value of emancipation. After issuing a preliminary emancipation in September 1862, Lincoln signed the Emancipation

Proclamation on January 1, 1863, freeing slaves in areas that remained under Confederate control (Document 1). African Americans and their abolitionist allies rejoiced, as did congressional Radical Republicans, who had tirelessly insisted that the war for Union must also be a war against slavery. Congress had done its part, passing a bill to outlaw slavery in the District of Columbia and several measures allowing Union armies to confiscate rebel slave property. Radical congressmen were also in constant contact with Lincoln. They advocated immediate and unconditional emancipation, and did not hesitate to criticize the commander in chief when he seemed to be dragging his feet. As Radical representative George Julian somewhat self-servingly explained in his memoirs, "It was in yielding to this pressure that [Lincoln] finally became the liberator of the slaves."[18] Wherever the credit belonged, it is clear that the Emancipation Proclamation marked an important turning point. From this moment, the Union armies would act as de facto agents of emancipation, the American flag becoming—finally—a symbol of freedom. Meanwhile, the Proclamation ensured that the status of millions of formerly enslaved African Americans would be a central concern animating any proposal for the postwar South.[19]

Lincoln presented a plan for Reconstruction in December 1863. In his Proclamation of Amnesty and Reconstruction, Lincoln offered a pardon to southerners willing to pledge future loyalty and to accept emancipation. When 10 percent of a state's voting population had taken the prescribed loyalty oath, this group would be eligible to form a new state government and to re-establish relations with the United States. The plan stipulated that the reconstituted states must abolish slavery, but otherwise it said very little about the fate of the freedpeople (Document 2). Lincoln's Ten Percent Plan was, above all, a wartime plan for Reconstruction. As some critics pointed out, 10 percent of a state's population hardly constituted an overwhelming expression of loyalty. Lincoln's aim, however, was to entice anti-Confederate southerners to return to the Union with the express goal of shortening the war. As much a war measure as a Reconstruction program, the Ten Percent Plan may not have been Lincoln's final word on Reconstruction.[20]

In July 1864, congressional Republicans offered their own program for Reconstruction. The Wade-Davis Bill, named for its sponsors, Benjamin Wade and Maryland representative Henry Winter Davis, was a self-conscious alternative to the leniency of Lincoln's Ten Percent Plan. Rather than 10 percent, the Wade-Davis Bill required a majority of a state's white men to sign a loyalty oath before the readmission process could commence. In choosing delegates to the conventions that would then redraft the state constitutions, suffrage would be limited to those men who could take the so-called Ironclad Oath: a pledge that one had never voluntarily aided the Confederacy. The Wade-Davis Bill also mandated legal equality for the freedpeople, a provision absent in Lincoln's plan. Fearful that the Wade-Davis Bill would disrupt wartime Reconstruction efforts already under way in Louisiana, Lincoln simply refused to sign it (a procedure known as a pocket veto). Furious, Wade and Davis issued a manifesto sharply critical of Lincoln's actions and his Reconstruction policy (Document 3).

This split between Lincoln and congressional Radicals presaged two debates that would resurface time and again in the postwar years. First, the disagreement suggested that the proper location of federal power was not entirely clear. Who should have control over Reconstruction, Congress or the president? The U.S. Constitution, which did not imagine the eventuality of a civil war (let alone Reconstruction), offered no guidance. This question of jurisdiction would become a full-blown crisis once Andrew Johnson assumed the presidency. Second, the competing wartime plans highlighted an important division over the larger purpose of Reconstruction. Was Reconstruction simply a matter of restoration, or must it produce deeper, long-lasting change in the South? Lincoln's was a plan for restoration. Wade and Davis sought to create a new South. This distinction would prove extraordinarily significant in the years to come.

Despite their differences, Lincoln worked with congressional Republicans to pass the Thirteenth Amendment to the U.S. Constitution in early 1865. The amendment, ratified by the states late in the year, outlawed "slavery and involuntary servitude" in the United States, placing emancipation on a secure and permanent footing. The amendment guaranteed that, whatever the results of Reconstruction, it would never again be legal for one person to own another (Document 4). Beyond this, however, the amendment left many questions unanswered. It enshrined the principle of freedom in the Constitution, but it said nothing about the rights and privileges that came with that freedom. The legal and political status of the freedpeople in the postwar nation remained an open question.[21]

ANDREW JOHNSON AND THE RADICALS

The assassination of Abraham Lincoln in April 1865 instantly changed the face of the Reconstruction process. Although there is no way to know how Lincoln's Reconstruction policy would have shifted over time—his thinking on emancipation had certainly evolved during the war—Radicals had ample reason to believe that his successor, Andrew Johnson, would adopt a southern policy that more closely aligned with their own viewpoint. Although he was a white southerner himself, Johnson's impoverished upbringing had instilled in him an intense dislike of the South's landed aristocracy. In 1864, Johnson had declared that "Treason must be made odious, and traitors must be punished and impoverished."[22] Such words were music to Radical ears, suggesting that Johnson would be amenable to the sort of far-reaching, transformative Reconstruction that they advocated. As Radical representative George Julian recalled in his memoir, "The feeling was nearly universal that the ascension of Johnson to the Presidency would prove a godsend to the country."[23] Subsequent events would prove this confidence misplaced.

Having adjourned in March 1865, Congress did not come back into session until December. For almost nine months, therefore, federal Reconstruction policy was President Johnson's domain. In spite of his bold talk of punishing traitors, Johnson's vision of Reconstruction had little in common with that of the Radicals. Believing that secession was impossible and that the South had never truly left the United States, Johnson saw Reconstruction as a simple matter of restoring the ex-Confederate states to their former status within the nation. Beyond this, Johnson disagreed fundamentally with the Radicals' broad notion of federal power, particularly the powers of Congress. Finally, Johnson was a former Democrat and avowed white supremacist who had little commitment to the welfare of southern freedpeople. His Reconstruction program—often referred to as "Presidential Reconstruction"—would reflect these beliefs.

In late May 1865, Johnson issued a pair of proclamations that laid out his Reconstruction policy. Johnson's vision of Reconstruction was, in many ways, similar to that put forward in Lincoln's Ten Percent Plan. The first proclamation pardoned the vast majority of participants in the rebellion. For most white southerners, amnesty would require only a simple oath pledging loyalty to the Union and acceptance of emancipation. Fourteen classes, including the leadership of the Confederacy and the region's wealthiest landowners, were excluded from the proclamation and were required to apply individually for a pardon. The second proclamation established a policy for the readmission of the southern states. Johnson appointed a provisional governor for the state of North Carolina and invited residents to call a convention for the purpose of rewriting the state constitution. With the exception of those classes explicitly denied a pardon, all persons eligible to vote before secession—and *only* those persons—would vote for convention delegates. This meant, of course, that African American suffrage would not be part of Presidential Reconstruction. The policy enacted with reference to North Carolina was quickly expanded to the rest of the Confederacy (Document 6).

White southern conservatives soon came to recognize that they had an unexpected ally in Johnson. The changes that Reconstruction brought about might not be as far-reaching as they had feared. Johnson's policy allowed them great leeway in shaping the transition from war to Reconstruction and left the status of the freedpeople in the hands of the white South. Throughout the summer of 1865, Johnson approved thousands of individual pardons for white southerners excluded from the general amnesty. During the same months, the southern states elected delegates for their constitutional conventions, which would meet in the fall. The documents these conventions produced were required to acknowledge emancipation, reject the doctrine of secession, and void Confederate debts. Otherwise, Johnson left the states to manage their own affairs. With new constitutions in hand, the former Confederate states were free to hold elections to fill state and national offices. Although Johnson had hoped that his policies would foster the growth of a new leadership class in the South, the congressmen elected in the fall of 1865 included several Confederate generals and Alexander Stephens, vice president of the Confederacy. Such an unapologetic embrace of the old order caused deep concern among many northerners.[24]

The so-called Black Codes that the reconvened southern legislatures began to pass in late 1865 posed an even greater problem. In order to secure a stable and inexpensive plantation labor force after the demise of slavery, the new legislatures of the former Confederacy turned to patently discriminatory legislation. While specifics varied by state, the Black Codes curbed African Americans' freedom of movement, limited their ability to choose employment, imposed harsh penalties for a variety of real or imagined offenses, and established an "apprenticeship" system that provided white landowners with the labor of black minors, free of charge. Other laws limited black access to schools, transportation, and public services. Johnson had allowed the southern states to regulate their own internal affairs. In response, southern legislatures set about reproducing the racial inequalities of slavery in an age of freedom (Document 12).

During Johnson's first months in office, the Reconstruction program enjoyed wide northern support. The leniency of Johnson's "May Proclamations" horrified the Radicals, but moderate and conservative

Republicans rallied behind him (Documents 7, 8, and 9). By the year's end, however, northern popular opinion had begun to shift. The clear discriminatory intent of the Black Codes forced many northerners to conclude that further guarantees of African American civil rights were necessary. If the southern states could not be relied upon to deal fairly with the freedpeople, the federal government would have to step in. From Johnson's perspective, however, Reconstruction had largely run its course by December 1865. In his annual message to Congress, Johnson expressed his satisfaction. Southern state governments were now in place, governing under new constitutions that outlawed slavery and denied the legality of secession. Further changes in southern race relations, Johnson argued, would emanate from the states, not from Washington. Congress had only to admit the new southern members and to begin the work of governance in a reunited nation. The work of "restoration"—Johnson's preferred term—was largely complete (Document 14).

Congressional Republicans had other ideas. They recognized that any chance to protect African American civil rights by federal enactment would dissolve as soon as southern congressmen reclaimed their seats. Since the U.S. Constitution guarantees each house of Congress the right to judge the qualifications of its own members, congressional Republicans simply refused to recognize the newly arrived southern contingent. Having halted Johnson's "restoration," congressional Radicals quickly called for black suffrage, a program of land redistribution, and the nullification of the state governments established under Presidential Reconstruction (Documents 15 and 16). At this point, however, a more moderate view of Reconstruction predominated among Republicans. In early 1866, Illinois moderate Lyman Trumbull introduced two bills in the Senate. The first bill proposed to continue support for the Freedmen's Bureau, a federal body founded in 1865 to assist the formerly enslaved in their transition to freedom. The second piece of legislation was a Civil Rights Bill that expanded the boundaries of American citizenship to include African Americans and defined the rights owed to all citizens, including the right to contract freely and the right to sue in a court of law. Trumbull's bill was a direct response to the systematic racial discrimination practiced under the Johnson governments and manifested in the Black Codes. Although congressional moderates like Trumbull were not yet ready to overturn Johnson's work, they saw the Civil Rights Bill as a necessary supplement to Presidential Reconstruction. It was a bulwark against inequality and an affirmation that black freedom carried with it certain fundamental rights (Documents 17 and 18).

When the Freedmen's Bureau Bill and the Civil Rights Bill (Document 19) passed Congress with wide Republican support, most commentators assumed that Johnson would sign both bills. They were mistaken. Johnson vetoed the Freedmen's Bureau Bill, sending a veto message to Congress that sharply criticized the wisdom of federal interventionism on behalf of southern African Americans. His veto of the Civil Rights Bill made the split permanent (Document 20). Although Johnson's motivation for the vetoes remains uncertain — his own reelection plans and his unwavering belief in white supremacy certainly played a role — their meaning was unmistakable. Given the relative moderation of both of Trumbull's bills, it seemed clear that Johnson was likely to veto every piece of congressional legislation dealing with the South. To accomplish anything, congressional Republicans would need to muster the two-thirds majority of both houses required to overturn a presidential veto. In April, they did just that, passing the Civil Rights Bill over Johnson's veto (Document 21). Congressional Republicans now recognized that Johnson was not an ally in their attempt to reform the South. He was their most powerful adversary.

THE FOURTEENTH AMENDMENT AND THE ELECTION OF 1866

For all it accomplished, the Civil Rights Bill did not amount to a plan for Reconstruction. Refusing to seat the southern claimants in December 1865 had allowed Congress time to pass civil rights legislation, but all recognized that this exclusion could only be temporary. Eventually, the southern states would have to be readmitted to Congress. Before they could be, however, a number of troubling questions would need to be addressed. Most pressing was the continued violation of black civil rights across the South. White-on-black violence remained distressingly common. A brutal massacre in Memphis, Tennessee, in May 1866 dramatized the need for further federal action to protect the lives and livelihoods of southern freedpeople (Document 22). Though the Civil Rights Bill had been an important step, congressional Republicans hoped to put the civil rights of black southerners on firmer ground. Shifting partisan majorities could overturn a piece of legislation; a constitutional amendment guaranteeing equal protection under the law would secure black rights in perpetuity (Document 23).

Southern suffrage regulations posed another crucial dilemma. In an ironic twist, the white South actually stood to *gain* seats in Congress because newly freed African Americans—now recognized as full citizens—added to the state population totals by which congressional seats were delegated. If this gain were not offset by the advent of black suffrage, southern whites would benefit politically. Radicals argued that providing the vote to the freedpeople would solve the problem. Moderate and conservative Republicans, however, were not yet prepared for this step. Some other remedy would need to be devised. The political status of former Confederates was also up for debate. Should traitors and secessionists be allowed to vote and to hold office? Or should Congress impose some sort of restriction in an attempt to create a healthier political climate in the South?

Out of these debates grew the Fourteenth Amendment to the Constitution. The amendment enshrined equality before the law in the Constitution and established the federal government as a defender of this principle. In so doing, the amendment reimagined the nature of citizenship and altered the relationship between American citizens and their government. In its final form, the Fourteenth Amendment contained five sections. The most important section was the first, which affirmed the provisions of the Civil Rights Bill, defining citizenship and preventing the states from violating the "privileges and immunities" of its citizens, regardless of race. The second section addressed the suffrage issue, reducing congressional representation for states that denied the vote to any portion of their male citizens. This was a compromise measure, which allowed Congress to avoid the issue of black suffrage. As originally written, the third section temporarily denied the right to vote to former Confederates. Bowing to moderate pressure, however, the section was rewritten to limit Confederate office-holding, with no restrictions placed on suffrage. The fourth section addressed Confederate war debt, and the fifth section empowered Congress to enforce the provisions of the amendment. The amendment was the logical culmination of congressional efforts up to this point, marking the fulfillment of the Republican party's commitment to civil rights and legal equality (Document 25).[25]

Although it passed with near universal Republican support in both houses, many leading Radicals in Congress felt that the amendment did not go far enough. Charles Sumner sharply criticized the amendment's failure to address black male suffrage. Thaddeus Stevens considered it a betrayal of the Radicals' dream of racial equality. Rather than working to build a truly democratic nation, Stevens complained, "I find that we shall be obliged to be content with patching up the worst portions of the ancient edifice" (Document 24).[26] Outside of Congress, Radical sympathizers roundly criticized the amendment. Abolitionist Wendell Phillips was incensed that the amendment stopped short of black suffrage, calling it a "fatal and total surrender" (Document 26).[27] Susan B. Anthony and Elizabeth Cady Stanton, leading advocates of women's suffrage, opposed the amendment because its second section specifically referred to "male citizens." In using this language, Congress gave its consent to the continued denial of women's voting rights. From the perspective of Radicals and Radical sympathizers, therefore, the Fourteenth Amendment was, at best, a compromise measure.

The Fourteenth Amendment became the central issue in the congressional midterm elections of 1866. Congressional Republicans entered the election season in a strong position, having fulfilled the popular mandate for legal equality while avoiding the much more controversial issue of black suffrage. Although Andrew Johnson was not up for reelection, he spent the fall of 1866 diligently working to oust as many of his congressional enemies as possible. In late August, Johnson embarked on a northern speaking tour, in which he attacked congressional Reconstruction policy, questioned the power of the federal government, and insisted that issues of suffrage be left to the states. Unfortunately for his cause, however, Johnson also made a number of more intemperate statements. At one stop, he seemed to advocate the hanging of Thaddeus Stevens; at another, he compared himself to Jesus Christ.[28] Between Johnson's questionable judgment and the broad popularity of Congress's handling of Reconstruction, the Republicans scored a smashing victory in the elections of 1866. When Congress reconvened the next year, Republicans would enjoy majorities in both houses large enough to easily override Johnson's vetoes.

The question was how white southerners would respond. In late 1866 the Fourteenth Amendment went before the states for ratification. Although Congress had adjourned without establishing a clear policy on the matter, it was apparent that ratification would be a minimum requirement for the readmission of the southern states and the seating of their congressional contingents. And yet, one by one, the southern state legislatures refused to ratify. With the lone exception of Tennessee, each of the states of the former Confederacy rejected the amendment by a large majority. Their stubborn refusal to accept the mandate of Congress would have enormous political ramifications. In failing to ratify the Fourteenth Amendment, southern state legislatures empowered the Radical forces in Washington, daring Congress to take further steps and all but guaranteeing the advent of black suffrage (Document 28).

THE RECONSTRUCTION ACT OF 1867

When Congress reconvened in December 1866, it appeared that the hour of Radical Republicanism had dawned. With the nearly universal rejection of the Fourteenth Amendment—the crown jewel of moderate Republicanism—by the legislatures of the southern states, even committed moderates such as Senator Lyman Trumbull found themselves gravitating toward the political program of the Radicals. While the South's failure to ratify the Fourteenth Amendment weighed heavily on the minds of congressional Republicans, they faced a much more pressing crisis. Simply put, the lives of African Americans and white Republicans were not secure in the South. From a variety of sources, reports came of the severity and ubiquity of southern racial violence. Northern travel writers and journalists published gruesome descriptions of politically motivated bloodshed. Agents of the Freedmen's Bureau filled their reports with tales of murder and terror. When the perpetrators of violence were brought to trial, local juries frequently refused to convict white men for attacks on the freedpeople. In many parts of the South, a systematic campaign of violence and intimidation kept African Americans locked in low-paying agricultural labor and prevented them from exercising the most basic prerogatives of citizenship. The Civil Rights Bill meant little if those in power completely ignored its dictates. Reconstruction appeared to have gone off the rails.[29]

It is in this context that a majority of congressional Republicans came to believe that a period of federal oversight of the South was the only way to redeem the region. They sought, in effect, to start the Reconstruction process over. They argued that Andrew Johnson's leniency had done the nation a grave disservice. The state governments elected under Presidential Reconstruction showed no interest in protecting the freedpeople or in obeying congressional civil rights legislation. Congressional Republicans insisted that state sovereignty should have been withheld until racial violence had ceased and African American rights had been secured. They believed, however, that the federal government had the power to undo Johnson's mistakes. Congress could place the South under federal rule until a more healthful political culture had taken root. In the meantime, the U.S. military would keep order in the region. Armed with a veto-proof majority and overwhelming popular support, congressional Republicans hoped to secure fundamental and lasting change in the former Confederacy. They would start from the beginning, giving themselves a second chance to get Reconstruction right (Documents 34 and 35).

At the heart of the new Reconstruction program was African American suffrage. Committed Radicals like Sumner and Stevens had long insisted that freedmen deserved the right to vote. By early 1867, however, black suffrage had become an article of faith for most Republicans. While the bill that would eventually become the Reconstruction Act of 1867 produced significant debate within Congress, the provisions regarding African American male suffrage were largely uncontroversial. By including the South's African Americans in the region's political process, Republican congressmen sought to empower the freedmen to help themselves. Southern state governments were likely to be much more interested in the protection of black civil rights when African Americans possessed the vote and, therefore, the ability to remove unreceptive politicians from office. Republicans had great faith in the power of black suffrage. According to the prevailing logic, black voters would sweep unrepentant rebels from office, replacing them with progressive leaders capable of guiding the South to a brighter future. In so doing, they would lead the way to the speedy and honorable resolution of the Reconstruction process. Of course, the fact that African American voters proved extremely loyal to the Republican party was also a consideration. Largely thanks to the pressing reality of southern violence, black suffrage had gone from Radical dream to national policy in a remarkably short period of time (Documents 32 and 33).

The Reconstruction Act of 1867, passed in early March over Johnson's veto, placed the former Confederacy (except Tennessee) under the control of the U.S. Army. It split the region into five military districts, putting army personnel in charge of each. In the absence of reliable civil authorities, the military was tasked with keeping order. This arrangement was purely temporary, however. The act also laid out the steps by which new state governments were to be organized. Each of the states of the former Confederacy (except Tennessee, which had already been readmitted to Congress) was instructed to organize a constitutional convention. African Americans were eligible to vote for convention delegates, and the constitutions that the conventions prepared were required to include a provision legalizing black suffrage. The act barred leading Confederates from voting for delegates to the state constitutional conventions, though it did not impose any further limits on Confederate suffrage. When a state had approved its new constitution and ratified the Fourteenth Amendment, military control would be lifted and the new state government recognized by Congress (Document 36). The conventions charged with redrafting the southern state constitutions began meeting in the fall.

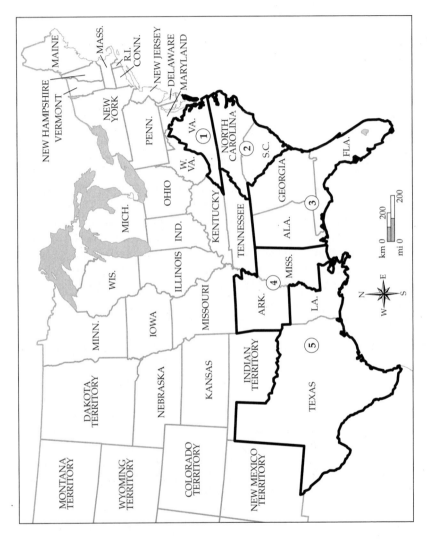

Map 1. *Reconstruction Military Districts.*

By the middle of 1867, southern African Americans had begun registering to vote and casting their first ballots (Document 37). Since emancipation, freedpeople had displayed a high degree of political organization and energy. Joining groups such as the Union League, southern African Americans debated the great social and economic questions of the age—race relations, Reconstruction policy, land redistribution, female suffrage. Black southern mobilization often followed lines established during slavery, with existing religious and community structures repurposed as sites of electoral politics. Former slaves imagined a society where all were treated equally, regardless of race. As an Alabama freedmen's convention put it, "we claim exactly *the same rights, privileges and immunities as are enjoyed by white men*—we ask nothing more and will be content with nothing less."[30] For southern African Americans, this was the meaning of Radical Reconstruction. Freedmen voted in large numbers and held a variety of local, state, and national offices during Reconstruction. Sixteen African Americans served in the U.S. House of Representatives and the Senate (Documents 50 and 51).[31] They were, without exception, members of the Republican party. The Reconstruction Act revolutionized the southern polity, creating—for the first time in the region's history—a genuine biracial democracy.[32]

THE IMPEACHMENT OF ANDREW JOHNSON AND THE ELECTION OF ULYSSES S. GRANT

The Reconstruction Act would be the high-water mark of congressional Radicalism. In its embrace of military rule and its introduction of black suffrage, the Reconstruction Act was a truly remarkable document. Perhaps for this reason, many non-Radical Republicans treated it as the final piece of congressional Reconstruction. Having replaced the southern state governments and empowered the freedmen with the vote, many congressional Republicans assumed that the legislative framework of Reconstruction was fully in place. Although stalwarts like Charles Sumner and George Julian would continue to urge action on issues like land redistribution, the aftermath of the Reconstruction Act saw a decline in legislative activism (Document 38).

Along with much of the American public, congressional Republicans spent late 1867 and early 1868 wondering what to do about Andrew Johnson. For two years, Johnson had been a committed opponent of Reconstruction who had sought, at every turn, to undo congressional policy in the South. Many congressional Republicans had come to believe that Johnson was perilously close to destroying everything for which they had worked. The Reconstruction Act had placed the South temporarily under the jurisdiction of the military, which the president, as commander in chief, controlled. In effect, Congress had placed Johnson at the head of its Reconstruction effort in the South. Throughout 1867, Johnson did what he could to foil congressional aims, advancing a narrow reading of the Reconstruction Act and limiting the scope of military oversight. When an impeachment motion failed to pass the House of Representatives late in 1867, Johnson accelerated his efforts to sabotage Reconstruction from the inside (Document 40). He replaced a number of Radical-leaning military officials in the South with conservatives, lending support to anti-Reconstruction forces. Congressional Republicans passed several supplementary bills designed to protect their Reconstruction program, but Johnson seemed to have the law on his side.

To truly undo the work of Reconstruction, however, Johnson would have to dispense with Edwin M. Stanton, the secretary of war. Much to Johnson's dismay, Stanton tended to side with Congress on most political issues. With a supportive secretary of war and a coterie of like-minded generals in charge across the South, Johnson would have been able to do very serious damage to the Reconstruction project, effectively nullifying the military as a protective force. In March 1867, however, Congress had passed the Tenure of Office Act, a piece of legislation designed to protect Republican political appointees from Johnson's power of removal. One of the Tenure of Office Act's provisions required the Senate to approve the dismissal of cabinet members (including the secretary of war) during the term of the president who had appointed them (Document 41).[33] During the summer of 1867, Johnson had taken advantage of a congressional recess to suspend Secretary Stanton. Late in the year, he sought to make the removal permanent. However, in January 1868, the Senate rejected the dismissal. Fearing that his frontal assault on the Reconstruction Act was in danger, Johnson persisted. A little more than a month later, he announced the removal of Stanton, in violation of the terms of the Tenure of Office Act. Johnson's illegal dismissal of Stanton unified Republican forces in Congress.

On March 2, 1868, the House of Representatives approved eleven articles of impeachment, most of them directly related to the removal of Edwin Stanton (Document 42). Throughout April and into May, the House impeachment managers presented their evidence to the Senate. In late May, the Senate voted to acquit the president. Thirty-five senators—one short of the two-thirds required for conviction—voted to convict, but seven Republicans crossed party lines to support the president (Document 43).[34] As the lack of party unanimity suggests, the impeachment of Johnson was a desperate gamble; it may also have been congressional Republicans' gravest mistake.

A number of factors contributed to the failure of the impeachment proceedings. First of all, had the Senate voted to remove Johnson, Radical senator Benjamin Wade would have become president (since Johnson had not appointed a vice president, Wade, as president pro tempore of the Senate, would have been next in line). Wade's Radicalism troubled many moderate and conservative Republicans, as did the fact that he declined to remove himself from the impeachment proceedings in spite of his personal stake in conviction. Second, Johnson's allies assured Republican senators that the president would stop his attack on congressional Reconstruction should he be allowed to remain in office. Third, no matter how much they disliked Johnson personally or politically, Republican senators recognized the gravity of the situation. This was the first presidential impeachment in the nation's history. A conviction would have set an important precedent, and some senators found the case against Johnson wanting. Finally, there was the simple fact that the articles of impeachment did not address Johnson's real failings as president. Johnson was stubborn, proud, underhanded, and totally lacking in political savvy and leadership qualities. For two years he had worked to undercut congressional policy, putting the success of the Reconstruction endeavor and the fate of the freedpeople in very real jeopardy. These actions, however, did not constitute grounds for impeachment. Instead, the case against Johnson was a formal and legalistic one, centered on the Tenure of Office Act and the dismissal of Stanton. Johnson may have deserved removal, but the House impeachment managers failed to produce charges that would have justified this drastic step.

In the wake of the impeachment trial, the nation's attention turned to the presidential election of 1868. General Ulysses S. Grant, who had led the victorious Union armies during the Civil War, was the obvious choice to receive the Republican nomination. Members of the party's Radical wing expressed some concern over Grant's political moderation, but they could not deny his appeal with the populace. The Democrats nominated former New York governor Horatio Seymour, who ran a campaign almost entirely devoted to opposition to Reconstruction (Document 46). In November, Grant won handily, largely thanks to the votes of newly enfranchised southern freedmen. In the run-up to the election, Grant had promised to restore order and goodwill to the fractured nation, famously imploring, "Let us have peace" (Document 45). But in the South, racial violence was quickly reaching epidemic proportions. Grant was repeatedly forced to deploy troops to protect the lives and rights of southern Republicans. Throughout his presidency, Grant struggled to stabilize a South that seemed enmeshed in a semi-permanent state of war.[35]

FROM RADICALISM TO REDEMPTION

The failure of the impeachment trial and the election of the moderate Republican Grant foretold the end of congressional Radicalism, but one important move remained. Republicans recognized that so long as black suffrage was enshrined only at the state level, it remained insecure. In late 1868, Republicans began debate on one more proposed constitutional amendment. The Fifteenth Amendment prohibited the states from denying the right to vote to any citizen on the basis of "race, color, or previous condition of servitude." Technically, the Fifteenth Amendment did not provide southern African Americans with any rights that were not already promised in the new state constitutions produced under the auspices of the Reconstruction Act of 1867. Even so, the amendment was significant for at least three reasons. First of all, it extended African American suffrage to the states of the North. Second, it enshrined voting rights in the Constitution, protecting the suffrage against future attempts to restrict it. Third, it served an important symbolic purpose, nationalizing the commitment to racial equality and providing a capstone to Republican Reconstruction. The Fifteenth Amendment passed Congress on February 26, 1869, and was ratified by the states a year later (Documents 47 and 48). Together, the so-called Reconstruction Amendments—the Thirteenth, barring slavery; the Fourteenth, defining citizenship and establishing legal equality; and the Fifteenth, guaranteeing the right to vote regardless of race—forever changed the U.S. Constitution.

Largely thanks to the votes of African Americans, Republican regimes won control of state governments throughout the former Confederacy following the passage of the Reconstruction Act. Almost immediately, however, conservative Democrats began a campaign to regain the political upper hand. By reclaiming governorships and securing legislative majorities within the southern states, Democrats hoped to limit the impact of federal Reconstruction policies. This process was called "Redemption." When legitimate political means proved insufficient, white southern Democrats turned to violence. By 1868, an organization called the Ku Klux Klan had begun to terrorize black and white Republicans across the South. During its infamous night rides, the Klan resorted to torture, rape, and murder to carry out its political agenda. Federal enforcement legislation passed in 1870 and 1871 effectively destroyed the Ku Klux Klan, but a variety of related paramilitary organizations (including the White League and the Red Shirts) quickly arose to take its place. Working through legitimate political channels and through terrorist violence, southern Democrats dedicated themselves to the overthrow of Reconstruction (Documents 52 and 53).[36]

By 1876, they had largely succeeded. As that year's fall elections approached, only three southern states—Louisiana, South Carolina, and Florida—remained in Republican control. The presidential election pitted Republican governor Rutherford B. Hayes of Ohio against Democratic governor Samuel J. Tilden of New York. Hayes was declared the victor in an extraordinarily close and controversial election, but the Democrats secured the governorships in each of the unredeemed southern states. With that, the Redemption of the South was complete, and Reconstruction was, for all intents and purposes, over. While he remained committed to protecting African American rights, Hayes shunned the political and military interventionism of the Grant administration, working hard to conciliate the white South. Hayes's southern policy horrified those who remained committed to racial egalitarianism in the South. However, northern Republicans who had grown weary of the "southern question" embraced Hayes's call to transcend the sectional politics of Reconstruction (Document 54).[37]

Into the 1880s, African Americans continued to vote and hold public office across the South. By the early 1890s, however, southern white Democrats had had enough. Seeking to dismantle what remained of the Reconstruction racial order and to secure the ascendancy of white supremacy, they constructed the system that would come to be known as Jim Crow. Over the next two decades, southern states segregated public space and passed restrictive legislation to deny black voting rights. White mobs lynched thousands of African Americans in a brutal show of force. Although these activities were in obvious violation of the Fourteenth and Fifteenth Amendments, the Republican party of the turn-of-the-century years had largely lost interest in the protection of black rights. The federal government failed to launch an effective response, dooming the egalitarian project of Reconstruction. Jim Crow segregation and the systematic denial of black suffrage reigned in the South until the civil rights movement of the mid-twentieth century.[38]

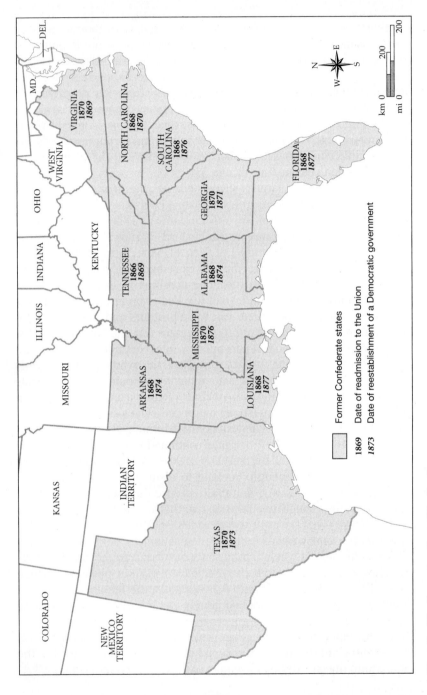

Map 2. *The Reconstruction of the South.*

26

As they constructed the apparatus of Jim Crow, southern propagandists also did their best to denigrate the memory of Radical Reconstruction. Presaging many of the arguments that would appear in Claude Bowers's *The Tragic Era*, late-nineteenth- and early-twentieth-century politicians, novelists, and historians cast Reconstruction as an era of vindictive legislation and unconstitutional federal overreach. To justify segregation and disfranchisement, defenders of Jim Crow needed to discredit the postwar era's great experiment in democracy and egalitarianism. Well into the twentieth century, most Americans accepted such misrepresentations as historical fact.[39]

THE LEGACY OF RADICAL RECONSTRUCTION

Congressional Republicans accomplished an enormous amount in their Reconstruction of the South. They destroyed slavery, protected African American civil rights, expanded the basis of citizenship, and established a clear program for the reincorporation of the former Confederate states into the nation. Perhaps most significant, Republican Reconstruction established a functioning biracial democracy in the South. Barely five years after emancipation, African Americans wielded the ballot across the region, while black politicians filled elective offices of every grade. Of course, more Radical programs, including widespread Confederate disfranchisement and the redistribution of southern land, never gained ground. While moderates within the Republican party had come to embrace civil equality and political equality, the issue of *economic* equality—the idea at the heart of the redistribution proposals—remained unaddressed. The failure to provide economic support left southern African Americans reliant on the vote alone. Congressional Republicans convinced themselves that in providing for black suffrage, they had armed the freedpeople with all the protection and support they needed. Subsequent events—from the violence of Redemption in the 1870s to the rise of Jim Crow in the 1890s—would prove them sadly mistaken.

With the benefit of hindsight, therefore, it is hard to deny that the Radical Republicans were remarkably perceptive. Alone among their Republican peers, they anticipated the scope and the scale of the white southern counterattack and did what they could to protect African American suffrage and citizenship. It may be that the Radicals had it right. Perhaps a more extreme Reconstruction policy—one that incorporated land redistribution, the territorialization of the southern states, and the long-term denial of Confederate voting rights—would have proven better able to withstand the onslaught of white supremacy. We will never know. As a practical matter, the political and social realities of the early postwar years made such a Reconstruction—a *truly* Radical Reconstruction—near impossible. Federal Reconstruction policy was a product of debate and negotiation on multiple levels: between Republican factions in Congress, between Congress and the president, between the federal government and southerners of both races.

In the end, it may be that the greatest legacy of the Radical Republicans was intellectual rather than political. Although many of their dreams would be deferred until the civil rights movement of the mid-twentieth century, the Radicals had the audacity to imagine a new nation, united in defense of equality, justice, and civil rights. They insisted that the federal government had both the power and the duty to aid and protect the weakest members of society. They sought to build a true democracy, one that respected and protected the civil and political rights of all, regardless of race. For the Radical Republicans, governance was fundamentally a moral issue. Rather than worrying about what was possible, Radicals sought to do what was right; they were less interested in what could be done than in what should be done. While many of their proposals went unimplemented and most of their accomplishments were quickly undermined or overthrown, the Radicals' egalitarian vision pointed the way to a more just and more democratic future.

NOTES

[1] Claude Bowers, *The Tragic Era: The Revolution after Lincoln* (Cambridge, Mass.: The Riverside Press, 1929), vi.

[2] Ibid., v.

[3] Ibid., v, vi.

[4] Ibid., 64.

[5] Bowers's view of Reconstruction was indebted to the work of William A. Dunning and his students at Columbia University. See John David Smith and J. Vincent Lowery, eds., *The Dunning School: Historians, Race, and the Meaning of Reconstruction* (Lexington: University Press of Kentucky, 2013). African American historians, notably W. E. B. Du Bois and John Hope Franklin, were among the first to critique interpretations like Bowers's. See W. E. B. Du Bois, *Black Reconstruction in America, 1860–1880* (1935, rpt.; New York: Free Press, 1999); John Hope Franklin, *Reconstruction after the Civil War* (1961; rpt., Chicago: University of Chicago Press, 1994). Since 1988, Eric Foner's interpretation of Reconstruction has become standard among historians. See Eric Foner, *Reconstruction: America's Unfinished Revolution, 1863–1877* (New York: Harper & Row, 1988).

[6] I have capitalized "Radical" throughout this volume whenever the word refers to the policies or personnel of the Radical Republicans.

[7] For an overview of Radical Republicanism, see Foner, *Reconstruction*, 228–80. See also Michael Les Benedict, *A Compromise of Principle: Congressional Republicans and Reconstruction, 1863–1869* (New York: W. W. Norton & Company, 1974).

[8] Cong. Globe, 38th Cong., 2nd Sess., 165.

[9] David Donald, *Charles Sumner and the Rights of Man* (New York: Random House, 1970).

[10] Hans L. Trefousse, *Thaddeus Stevens: Nineteenth-Century Egalitarian* (Chapel Hill: University of North Carolina Press, 1997).

[11] For an overview of Radical personnel, see Hans L. Trefousse, *The Radical Republicans: Lincoln's Vanguard for Racial Justice* (New York: Alfred A. Knopf, 1969).

[12] Foner, *Reconstruction*, 231.

[13] Richard Henry Dana, a Massachusetts jurist, laid out the "grasp of war" doctrine in a June 1865 speech. See Richard Henry Dana Jr., *Speeches in Stirring Times and Letters to a Son*, ed. Richard Henry Dana III (Boston: Houghton Mifflin, 1910), 234–72.

[14] Quoted in "Reconstruction," *New York Times*, 10 September 1865, 2.

[15] *The Works of Charles Sumner*, vol. X (Boston: Lee and Shepard, 1876), 56.

[16] Eric L. McKitrick, *Andrew Johnson and Reconstruction* (New York: Oxford University Press, 1960).

[17] Although it is beyond the scope of this volume to delve into the nature of southern politics during Reconstruction, a number of historians have undertaken this work. A small sample would include the following: Foner, *Reconstruction*, 77–123; Leon Litwack, *Been in the Storm So Long: The Aftermath of Slavery* (New York: Alfred A. Knopf, 1979); Michael Perman, *Reunion without Compromise: The South and Reconstruction, 1865–1868* (New York: Cambridge University Press, 1973); Steven Hahn, *A Nation under Our Feet: Black Political Struggles in the Rural South from Slavery to the Great Migration* (Cambridge, Mass.: Harvard University Press, 2005); Tera W. Hunter, *To 'Joy My Freedom: Southern Black Women's Lives and Labors after the Civil War* (Cambridge, Mass.: Harvard University Press, 1998); Paul Ortiz, *Emancipation Betrayed: The Hidden History of Black Organizing and White Violence in Florida from Reconstruction to the Bloody Election of 1920* (Berkeley: University of California Press, 2006).

[18] George W. Julian, *Political Recollections, 1840 to 1872* (Chicago: Jansen, McClurg & Company, 1884), 227.

[19] On Lincoln and emancipation, see Allen C. Guelzo, *Lincoln's Emancipation Proclamation: The End of Slavery in America* (New York: Simon & Schuster, 2006); Louis P. Masur, *Lincoln's Hundred Days: The Emancipation Proclamation and the War for Union* (Cambridge, Mass.: Harvard University Press, 2012). For a perspective that emphasizes the role that slaves played in pushing the nation toward emancipation, see Ira Berlin et al., *Slaves No More: Three Essays on Emancipation and the Civil War* (New York: Cambridge University Press, 1992).

[20] William C. Harris, *With Charity for All: Lincoln and the Restoration of the Union* (Lexington: University Press of Kentucky, 1999).

[21] Michael Vorenberg, *Final Freedom: The Civil War, the Abolition of Slavery, and the Thirteenth Amendment* (New York: Cambridge University Press, 2004).

[22] Foner, *Reconstruction*, 177.

[23] Julian, *Political Recollections*, 255.

[24] Dan T. Carter, *When the War Was Over: The Failure of Self-Reconstruction in the South, 1865–1867* (Baton Rouge: Louisiana State University Press, 1985).

[25] Garrett Epps, *Democracy Reborn: The Fourteenth Amendment and the Fight for Equal Rights in Post–Civil War America* (New York: Henry Holt, 2006).

[26] Cong. Globe, 39th Cong., 1st Sess., 3148.

[27] Foner, *Reconstruction*, 255.

[28] Edward McPherson, *Political History of the United States of America during the Period of Reconstruction* (Washington, D.C.: Philp & Solomons, 1871), 134–41.

[29] On racial violence in the Reconstruction South, see George C. Rable, *But There Was No Peace: The Role of Violence in the Politics of Reconstruction* (Athens: University of Georgia Press, 1984); Hannah Rosen, *Terror in the Heart of Freedom: Citizenship, Sexual Violence, and the Meaning of Race in the Postemancipation South* (Chapel Hill: University of North Carolina Press, 2009); Carole Emberton, *Beyond Redemption: Race, Violence, and the American South after the Civil War* (Chicago: University of Chicago Press, 2013).

[30] Foner, *Reconstruction*, 288.

[31] See ibid., 352–54; Eric Foner, *Freedom's Lawmakers: A Directory of Black Officeholders during Reconstruction* (Baton Rouge: Louisiana State University Press, 1996); Philip Dray, *Capitol Men: The Epic Story of Reconstruction through the Lives of the First Black Congressmen* (New York: Mariner Books, 2010).

[32] On black political activism in the Reconstruction South, see Foner, *Reconstruction*, 281–307; Hahn, *A Nation under Our Feet*, esp. 163–264; Ortiz, *Emancipation Betrayed*, 9–84.

[33] As a technical matter, it was not entirely clear whether this provision even applied to Stanton, who was a Lincoln appointee.

[34] Michael Les Benedict, *The Impeachment and Trial of Andrew Johnson* (New York: W. W. Norton & Company, 1973).

[35] Brooks D. Simpson, *The Reconstruction Presidents* (Lawrence: University Press of Kansas, 1998), 133–96; Foner, *Reconstruction*, 412–59.

[36] Allen W. Trelease, *White Terror: The Ku Klux Conspiracy and Southern Reconstruction* (New York: Harper and Row, 1972). See also Rable, *But There Was No Peace*; Emberton, *Beyond Redemption*.

[37] Simpson, *The Reconstruction Presidents*, 199–228.

[38] On the rise of Jim Crow, see Joel Williamson, *The Crucible of Race: Black-White Relations in the American South since Emancipation* (New York: Oxford University Press, 1984); Michael Perman, *Struggle for Mastery: Disfranchisement in the South, 1888–1908* (Chapel Hill: University of North Carolina Press, 2000); Grace Elizabeth Hale, *Making Whiteness: The Culture of Segregation in the South, 1890–1940* (New York: Vintage, 1999); Glenda Elizabeth Gilmore, *Gender and Jim Crow: Women and the Politics of White Supremacy in North Carolina, 1896–1920* (Chapel Hill: University of North Carolina Press, 1996); Crystal N. Feimster, *Southern Horrors: Women and the Politics of Rape and Lynching* (Cambridge, Mass.: Harvard University Press, 2009).

[39] Bruce E. Baker, *What Reconstruction Meant: Historical Memory in the American South* (Charlottesville: University of Virginia Press, 2007); David W. Blight, *Race and Reunion: The Civil War in American Memory* (Cambridge, Mass.: Harvard University Press, 2001); Smith and Lowery, eds., *The Dunning School*.

PART TWO

The Documents

1

Wartime Reconstruction and Presidential Reconstruction

1

ABRAHAM LINCOLN

The Emancipation Proclamation
January 1, 1863

In spite of his reputation as the "Great Emancipator," Abraham Lincoln arrived at a policy of emancipation slowly and cautiously. In embracing emancipation as a war policy, Lincoln responded to pressures on several fronts. Throughout 1861 and 1862, thousands of runaway slaves arrived at Union army encampments across the South. This flood of "contrabands" demanded a clear national policy on slavery. Lincoln also faced pressures from abolitionist and Radical Republican forces across the North, who urged him to turn a war for Union into a war for freedom. Finally, Lincoln recognized that slave labor was central to the Confederate war effort; emancipation would strike a powerful blow against the rebellion.

In September 1862, Lincoln issued a preliminary proclamation of emancipation. The document decreed that slaves in all parts of the Confederacy still in rebellion against the United States on January 1, 1863, would be free. True to his word, Lincoln issued the formal Emancipation Proclamation on New Year's Day, 1863. Although limited in its scope—note that slaves in Union-occupied areas in Virginia and Louisiana were not freed, nor were slaves in border states like Kentucky—the

From Edward McPherson, *The Political History of the United States of America during the Great Rebellion*, 2nd ed. (Washington, D.C.: Philp & Solomons, 1865), 228–29.

Emancipation Proclamation permanently changed the character of the Civil War. It opened the door to African American enlistment in the U.S. military, turned the U.S. Army into a force for freedom, and laid the groundwork for a post-slavery South.

I, ABRAHAM LINCOLN, President of the United States, by virtue of the power in me vested as Commander-in-Chief of the Army and Navy of the United States, in time of actual armed rebellion against the authority and Government of the United States, and as a fit and necessary war measure for suppressing said rebellion, do, on this first day of January, in the year of our Lord one thousand eight hundred and sixty-three, and in accordance with my purpose so to do, publicly proclaimed for the full period of one hundred days from the day first above mentioned, order and designate as the States and parts of States wherein the people thereof, respectively, are this day in rebellion against the United States, the following, to wit:

Arkansas, Texas, Louisiana, (except the parishes of St. Bernard, Plaquemines, Jefferson, St. John, St. Charles, St. James, Ascension, Assumption, Terre Bonne, Lafourche, St. Mary, St. Martin, and Orleans, including the city of New Orleans,) Mississippi, Alabama, Florida, Georgia, South Carolina, North Carolina, and Virginia, (except the forty-eight counties designated as West Virginia, and also the counties of Berkeley, Accomac, Northampton, Elizabeth City, York, Princess Ann, and Norfolk, including the cities of Norfolk and Portsmouth,) and which excepted parts are for the present left precisely as if this proclamation were not issued.

And by virtue of the power and for the purpose aforesaid, I do order and declare that all persons held as slaves within said designated States and parts of States are, and henceforward shall be, free; and that the Executive Government of the United States, including the military and naval authorities thereof, will recognize and maintain the freedom of said persons.

And I hereby enjoin upon the people so declared to be free to abstain from all violence, unless in necessary self-defence; and I recommend to them that, in all cases when allowed, they labor faithfully for reasonable wages.

And I further declare and make known that such persons, of suitable condition, will be received into the armed service of the United States to garrison forts, positions, stations, and other places, and to man vessels of all sorts in said service.

And upon this act, sincerely believed to be an act of justice, warranted by the Constitution upon military necessity, I invoke the considerate judgment of mankind and the gracious favor of Almighty God.

2

ABRAHAM LINCOLN

Proclamation of Amnesty and Reconstruction

December 8, 1863

In this proclamation, issued while the Civil War still raged, Abraham Lincoln began to sketch out a Reconstruction policy for the South. Lincoln's proclamation prescribed an oath by which white southerners could gain a pardon for their involvement with the Confederacy. When 10 percent of a state's eligible voters had taken the oath, this class would be empowered to create a new state government. Although Lincoln's proclamation excluded a number of classes from eligibility for a pardon—including former U.S. officeholders, high-ranking Confederate civil and military leaders, and those who had mistreated black and white Union prisoners of war—its leniency was striking. Aside from an acceptance of emancipation, which was non-negotiable, Lincoln's plan required relatively little from Confederates. It protected the right to all property (except slaves) and promised a speedy return to home rule in the South.

Like the Emancipation Proclamation, the Proclamation of Amnesty was a war measure. It was designed to encourage southerners to return to the Union as quickly as possible, thereby weakening the Confederacy. It is likely that the Ten Percent Plan would not have been Lincoln's final word on Reconstruction. In late 1863, however, Lincoln's priority was victory in the war. The Proclamation of Amnesty was a means to this end.

From Edward McPherson, *The Political History of the United States of America during the Great Rebellion*, 2nd ed. (Washington, D.C.: Philp & Solomons, 1865), 147.

I, ABRAHAM LINCOLN, President of the United States, do proclaim, declare, and make known to all persons who have directly, or by implication, participated in the existing rebellion, . . . that a full pardon is hereby granted to them and each of them, with restoration of all rights of property, except as to slaves, and in property cases where rights of third parties shall have intervened, and upon the condition that every such person shall take and subscribe an oath, and thenceforward keep and maintain said oath inviolate; and which oath shall be registered for permanent preservation, and shall be of the tenor and effect following, to wit:

"I, _____ _____, do solemnly swear, in presence of Almighty God, that I will henceforth faithfully support, protect, and defend the Constitution of the United States, and the union of the States thereunder; and that I will, in like manner, abide by and faithfully support all acts of Congress passed during the existing rebellion with reference to slaves, so long and so far as not repealed, modified, or held void by Congress, or by decision of the Supreme Court; and that I will, in like manner, abide by and faithfully support all proclamations of the President made during the existing rebellion having reference to slaves, so long and so far as not modified or declared void by decision of the Supreme Court. So help me God." . . .

And I do further proclaim, declare, and make known that whenever in any of the States of Arkansas, Texas, Louisiana, Mississippi, Tennessee, Alabama, Georgia, Virginia, Florida, South Carolina, and North Carolina, a number of persons, not less than one tenth in number of the votes cast in such State at the presidential election of the year of our Lord one thousand eight hundred and sixty, each having taken the oath aforesaid and not having since violated it, and being a qualified voter by the election law of the State existing immediately before the so-called act of secession, and excluding all others, shall re-establish a State government which shall be republican, and in nowise contravening said oath, such shall be recognized as the true government of the State, and the State shall receive thereunder the benefits of the constitutional provision which declares that "the United States shall guaranty to every State in this Union a republican form of government, and shall protect each of them against invasion; and, on application of the Legislature, or the Executive, (when the Legislature cannot be convened,) against domestic violence."

And I do further proclaim, declare, and make known that any provision which may be adopted by such State government in relation to the freed people of such State, which shall recognize and declare their permanent freedom, provide for their education, and which may yet be consistent, as a temporary arrangement, with their present condition as a laboring, landless, and homeless class, will not be objected to by the national Executive.

3

BENJAMIN WADE AND HENRY WINTER DAVIS

The Wade-Davis Manifesto

August 1864

Congressional Republicans were not entirely satisfied with Lincoln's Reconstruction program. In early July 1864, both houses of Congress approved a Reconstruction bill sponsored by Senator Benjamin Wade (Ohio) and Representative Henry Winter Davis (Maryland). The Wade-Davis Bill diverged from Lincoln's Ten Percent Plan in a number of important ways. The Wade-Davis Bill required a majority of white southerners in a state to sign a loyalty oath before the Reconstruction process could commence; Lincoln had required only 10 percent. The Wade-Davis Bill limited the suffrage to those white southerners who took an oath stating that they had never voluntarily aided the Confederacy; Lincoln's oath required only future loyalty to the United States. Perhaps most important, the Wade-Davis Bill suggested that Congress would control the course of Reconstruction; by his proclamation, Lincoln had implied that the president would shape southern policy.

When presented with the Wade-Davis Bill, Lincoln refused to sign it. Lincoln issued a proclamation explaining his "pocket veto," but congressional Radicals were incensed. Wade and Davis published a strongly worded "Manifesto" that critiqued Lincoln's actions, questioned his motivations, and made the case for the Wade-Davis Bill. They offered a number of comparisons between Lincoln's Reconstruction policy ("the proclamation") and the congressional approach ("the bill"). The

From Henry Winter Davis, *Speeches and Addresses Delivered in the Congress of the United States, and on Several Public Occasions* (New York: Harper & Brothers, 1867), 416, 423–25.

Wade-Davis Manifesto anticipated longer-term disagreements over the correct site of federal authority. At stake in this debate was a central question, one that would recur throughout the postwar era: Who would control Reconstruction, Congress or the president?

We have read without surprise, but not without indignation, the proclamation of the President of the 18th of July, 1864.[1] The supporters of the administration are responsible to the country for its conduct, and it is their right and duty to check the encroachments of the executive on the authority of Congress, and to require it to confine itself to the proper sphere. It is impossible to pass in silence this proclamation without neglecting that duty, and having taken as much responsibility as many others in supporting the administration, we are not disposed to fail in the other duty of supporting the rights of Congress. . . .

[W]hen we come to the guarantees of future peace which Congress meant to exact, the forms as well as the substance of the bill must yield to the President's will that none should be imposed. It was the solemn resolve of Congress to protect the loyal men of the nation against three great dangers: (1) the return to power of the guilty leaders of the rebellion; (2) the continuance of slavery; and (3) the burden of the rebel debt. Congress required assent to those provisions of the Convention of the State, and, if refused, it was to be dissolved. The President "holds for naught" that resolve of Congress, because he is unwilling "to be inflexibly committed to any one plan of restoration"; and the people of the United States are not to be allowed to protect themselves unless their enemies agree to it. The order to proceed according to the bill is therefore merely at the will of the rebel States, and they have the option to reject it and accept the proclamation of the 8th of December, and demand the President's recognition.[2] Mark the contrast! The bill requires a majority, the proclamation is satisfied with one tenth; the bill requires one oath, the proclamation another; the bill ascertains votes by registering, the proclamation by guess; the bill exacts adherence to existing territorial limits, the proclamation admits of others; the bill governs the rebel States *by law*, equalizing all before it, the proclamation commits them to the lawless discretion of military governors and

---

[1] Wade and Davis are here referring to Lincoln's proclamation explaining his pocket veto of the Wade-Davis Bill.

[2] They refer here to Lincoln's Proclamation of Amnesty and Reconstruction, in which he laid out the Ten Percent Plan.

provost-marshals; the bill forbids electors for President, the proclamation and defeat of the bill threaten us with civil war for the admission or exclusion of such votes; the bill exacted exclusion of dangerous enemies from power, and the relief of the nation from the rebel debt, and the prohibition of slavery forever, so that the suppression of the rebellion will double our resources to bear or pay the national debt, free the masses from the old domination of the rebel leaders, and eradicate the cause of the war; the proclamation secures neither of these guarantees.

It is silent respecting the rebel debt and the political exclusion of rebel leaders, leaving slavery exactly where it was by law at the outbreak of the rebellion, and adds no guarantees even of the freedom of the slaves the President undertook to manumit. It is summed up in an illegal oath, without a sanction, and therefore void. The oath is to support all proclamations of the President during the rebellion having reference to slaves. *Any* government is to be accepted at the hands of one tenth of the people not contravening that oath. Now that oath neither secures the abolition of slavery, nor adds any security to the freedom of the slaves whom the President declared free. It does not secure the abolition of slavery, for the proclamation of freedom merely professed to free certain slaves, while it recognized the institution. . . .

Such are the fruits of this rash and fatal act of the President, a blow at the friends of his administration, at the rights of humanity, and at the principles of republican government.

4

The Thirteenth Amendment to the U.S. Constitution

1865

The Thirteenth Amendment to the U. S. Constitution passed the Senate in late 1864 and the House of Representatives in early 1865. After ratification by three-quarters of the states, the amendment became a part of the Constitution in December 1865. The Thirteenth Amendment made the end of slavery permanent and irrevocable. Whereas Lincoln's

From Edward McPherson, *The Political History of the United States of America during the Period of Reconstruction* (Washington, D.C.: Philp & Solomons, 1871), 6.

Emancipation Proclamation was limited in geographical scope and open to future legal challenges, the Thirteenth Amendment placed a nationwide ban on "slavery and involuntary servitude" in the Constitution. Lincoln was a strong advocate of the amendment, working closely with congressional Republicans to secure its passage.

SEC. 1. Neither slavery nor involuntary servitude, except as a punishment for a crime, whereof the party shall have been duly convicted, shall exist within the United States, or any place subject to their jurisdiction.

SEC. 2. Congress shall have power to enforce this article by appropriate legislation.

5

REV. HENRY HIGHLAND GARNET

Speech on Racial Equality in the U.S. House of Representatives

February 12, 1865

About two weeks after the passage of the Thirteenth Amendment, Rev. Henry Highland Garnet became the first African American to deliver a speech in the chamber of the House of Representatives. Garnet, an escaped slave and committed abolitionist, was pastor of Fifteenth Street Presbyterian Church in Washington, D.C. Speaking on a Sunday, Garnet offered his listeners a religious sermon laced with political themes. He praised emancipation, but reminded the nation's politicians of the work that remained to be done. Garnet argued that political equality—including the right to vote—was the logical extension of the Union's policy of emancipation. While Garnet did not address the members of Congress directly, his speech offers a reminder of the extraordinarily significant role that African Americans played in urging the nation to adopt a policy of racial equality during the early days of Reconstruction.

A Memorial Discourse; by Rev. Henry Highland Garnet, Delivered in the Hall of the House of Representatives, Washington City, D.C. on Sabbath, February 12, 1865 (Philadelphia: Joseph M. Wilson, 1865), 85–87, 89–91.

It is often asked when and where the demands of the reformers of this and coming ages end? It is a fair question, and I will answer.

When all unjust and heavy burdens shall be removed from every man in the land. When all invidious and proscriptive distinctions shall be blotted out from our laws, whether they be constitutional, statute, or municipal laws. When emancipation shall be followed by enfranchisement, and all men holding allegiance to the government shall enjoy every right of American citizenship. When our brave and gallant soldiers shall have justice done to them. When the men who endure the sufferings and peril of the battle-field in defense of their country, and in order to keep our rulers in their places, shall enjoy the well-earned privilege of voting for them. When in the army and navy, and in every legitimate and honorable occupation, promotion shall smile upon merit without the slightest regard to the complexion of a man's face. When there shall be no more class-legislation, and no more trouble concerning the black man and his rights, than there is in regard to other American citizens. When, in every respect, he shall be equal before the law, and shall be left to make his own way in the social walks of life. . . .

We ask no special favors, but we plead for justice. While we scorn unmanly dependence; in the name of God, the universal Father, we demand the right to live, and labor, and to enjoy the fruits of our toil. . . .

Favored men, and honored of God as his instruments, speedily finish the work which he has given you to do. *Emancipate, Enfranchise, Educate, and give the blessings of the gospel to every American citizen.* . . .

Then before us a path of prosperity will open, and upon us will descend the mercies and favors of God. Then shall the people of other countries, who are standing tip-toe on the shores of every ocean, earnestly looking to see the end of this amazing conflict, behold a Republic that is sufficiently strong to outlive the ruin and desolations of civil war, having the magnanimity to do justice to the poorest and weakest of her citizens. Thus shall we give to the world the form of a model Republic, founded on the principles of justice, and humanity, and Christianity, in which the burdens of war and the blessings of peace are equally borne and enjoyed by all.

6

ANDREW JOHNSON

"May Proclamations"

May 29, 1865

When Abraham Lincoln was assassinated in April 1865, Vice President Andrew Johnson ascended to the presidency. With Congress out of session until December 1865, Johnson was free to steer federal Reconstruction policy as he saw fit. While many former Confederates feared the worst, Johnson's "May Proclamations" signaled to all observers that the president favored leniency and a speedy restoration of political rights. In his Proclamation of Amnesty, Johnson immediately pardoned most supporters of the Confederacy, restoring them to full political rights. Fourteen specially designated classes were excluded from the proclamation and were required to apply individually for amnesty. Throughout the summer and early fall of 1865, Andrew Johnson signed hundreds of pardons for high-ranking Confederate officials and large landowners disqualified from the general amnesty.

In a second proclamation, Johnson laid out the path by which former Confederate states could rejoin the Union. Although his initial proclamation referred exclusively to North Carolina, Johnson quickly issued similar orders relating to other parts of the Confederacy. Johnson chose a provisional governor for each state, instructing his appointees to call conventions to redraft the state constitutions. Johnson stipulated that those Confederates who had not yet received a pardon would be ineligible to vote for convention delegates, but otherwise the electorate of each state was to be identical to that which had voted for secession four years earlier. The freedmen would play no role in the political process. With their constitutions amended, the states of the South would be restored to their prewar status within the nation.

From Edward McPherson, *The Political History of the United States of America during the Period of Reconstruction* (Washington, D.C.: Philp & Solomons, 1871), 10–11.

Of Amnesty

I, Andrew Johnson, President of the United States, do proclaim and declare that I hereby grant to all persons who have, directly or indirectly, participated in the existing rebellion, except as hereinafter excepted, amnesty and pardon, with restoration of all rights of property, except as to slaves, and except in cases where legal proceedings, under the laws of the United States providing for the confiscation of property of persons engaged in the rebellion, have been instituted; but upon the condition, nevertheless, that every such person shall take and subscribe the following oath (or affirmation), and thenceforward keep and maintain said oath inviolate; and which oath shall be registered for permanent preservation, and shall be of the tenor and effect following, to wit:

"I, _____ _____, do solemnly swear (or affirm), in presence of Almighty God, that I will henceforth faithfully support, protect, and defend the Constitution of the United States, and the union of the States thereunder; and that I will, in like manner, abide by and faithfully support all laws and proclamations which have been made during the existing rebellion, with reference to the emancipation of slaves: So help me God."

The following classes of persons are excepted from the benefits of this proclamation:

1st. All who are or shall have been pretended civil or diplomatic or otherwise domestic or foreign agents of the pretended government.

2d. All who left judicial stations under the United States to aid the rebellion.

3d. All who shall have been military or naval officers of said pretended confederate government above the rank of colonel in the army, or lieutenant in the navy.

4th. All who left seats in the Congress of the United States to aid the rebellion. . . .

9th. All persons who held the pretended offices of governors of States in insurrection against the United States. . . .

13th. All persons who have voluntarily participated in said rebellion, and the estimated value of whose taxable property is over twenty thousand dollars. . . .

Provided, That special application may be made to the President for pardon by any person belonging to the excepted classes; and such clemency will be liberally extended as may be consistent with the facts of the case and the peace and dignity of the United States. . . .

Appointing William W. Holden Provisional Governor of North Carolina . . .

I, Andrew Johnson, President of the United States, and Commander-in-Chief of the army and navy of the United States, do hereby appoint William W. Holden Provisional Governor of the State of North Carolina, whose duty it shall be, at the earliest practicable period, to prescribe such rules and regulations as may be necessary and proper for convening a convention, composed of delegates to be chosen by that portion of the people of said State who are loyal to the United States, and no others, for the purpose of altering or amending the constitution thereof; and with authority to exercise, within the limits of said State, all the powers necessary and proper to enable such loyal people of the State of North Carolina to restore said State to its constitutional relations to the Federal Government, and to present such a republican form of State government as will entitle the State to the guarantee of the United States therefor, and its people to protection by the United States against invasion, insurrection, and domestic violence; *Provided*, that in any election that may be hereafter held for choosing delegates to any State convention, as aforesaid, no person shall be qualified as an elector, or shall be eligible as a member of such convention, unless he shall have previously taken the oath of amnesty, as set forth in the President's proclamation of May 29, A.D. 1865, and is a voter qualified as prescribed by the Constitution and laws of the State of North Carolina, in force immediately before the 20th day of May, 1861, the date of the so-called ordinance of secession; and the said convention when convened, or the Legislature that may be thereafter assembled, will prescribe the qualification of electors, and the eligibility of persons to hold office under the Constitution and laws of the State, a power the people of the several States composing the Federal Union have rightfully exercised from the origin of the Government to the present time.

7

GEORGE S. BOUTWELL

Speech on the "True Basis" of Reconstruction
July 4, 1865

George S. Boutwell was a Radical Republican representative from Massachusetts. In this speech, delivered in Weymouth, Massachusetts, Boutwell offered sharp criticism of Andrew Johnson's Reconstruction policies and laid out his own vision for the future of the South. The persistence of slavery, Boutwell argued, was the "great sin" of American history. The horrors of the Civil War had been a well-deserved punishment for generations of wrongdoing. Boutwell saw Reconstruction as an opportunity for the nation to recommit itself to the cause of justice. Reminding his listeners of the sacrifices made by black Union soldiers during the Civil War, Boutwell made an eloquent case for full African American citizenship and suffrage in the postwar era.

We have passed through a great struggle, which was a necessary incident of our national life, due to the fact, which now we can comprehend, and which it is neither disgrace to our fathers, nor dishonor to us, to confess, that our national system contained a fundamental error; namely, that it was possible to set up and maintain permanently a government based in part upon the principle that "all men are created equal," and in part upon the principle that a certain portion of mankind have the right to hold a certain other portion in bondage. . . .

Justice, *justice*, is the only foundation for statesmanship, the only security for national life; and our fathers, in departing from the principle of justice in the original construction of this government, left to their posterity the woes through which we have passed. Believing, as I do, that these horrors and sacrifices and suffering are a just judgment of Heaven upon this nation, for its great sin in reference to the institution of slavery, which is but one form of injustice, so here and everywhere during these four years I do pledge and have pledged myself

From George S. Boutwell, *Speeches and Papers Relating to the Rebellion and the Overthrow of Slavery* (Boston: Little, Brown, and Company, 1867), 372–73, 375–76, 403–4.

to resist the re-establishment of this government upon the principle of injustice. If there be those, few or many, who, in their anxiety to reconstruct their government speedily and according to its ancient forms, choose to forego the securities which ought to be taken, I have no lot or part with them. I prefer to stand alone, upon the principle of justice, as the only foundation on which the government can securely rest. And if there be those who choose to take the responsibility of becoming, in the eyes of posterity, the agents for the repetition of the woes which we have endured, let the responsibility be upon them. I feel assured, however, that whatever may be the prejudices of some, whatever may be the influence of tradition upon others, whatever may be the distinctions of race or color that exist among us, the people of this country are finally to re-establish the government upon the distinct enunciation of the doctrine that "all men are created equal." Building upon that foundation, the nation will withstand the storms and the floods of time: but if you build upon injustice, upon wrong, upon distinctions of race, of color, or upon caste, you build upon the sand; and when the storms come, and the winds blow, and the rains fall, then will the structure that you have reared be brought down in ruin upon your heads. . . .

You must be just to the negro. When you invited him to assume the uniform of the army of the republic, when you put the musket into his hand, when you asked him to jeopard,[1] and, if need be, to sacrifice, his life in defence of the country, you did in fact, if not in terms, agree, that, if the cause — his cause as well as your own — was successful, he should have the same part in the government as yourselves; and therefore you cannot, without the basest ingratitude, now reject him. I am compelled to declare to you, my friends, in all sincerity, heinous as are the crimes of these Southern men, infamous as they will be upon the page of history, that if the people of the North, now that they have acquired liberty for themselves, now that they have secured the restoration of the Union by the services and sacrifices of the negro in common with their own services and their own sacrifices, should surrender him, bound hand and foot, as he will be if he does not enjoy the right of suffrage, into the custody of his enemies, made doubly ferocious by the events of this war, and into the custody of your enemies also, your position upon the page of history, and in the judgment of posterity, will be only less infamous than theirs.

---

[1] To put in jeopardy.

8

THADDEUS STEVENS

Speech on Land Redistribution

September 6, 1865

Thaddeus Stevens, representative from Pennsylvania, was an acknowl-edged leader among congressional Radical Republicans. A devoted advocate of racial equality, Stevens was quick to criticize Andrew Johnson's Reconstruction policy for its failure to guarantee the civil rights of the South's freedpeople. In this address, delivered to his con-stituents in Lancaster, Pennsylvania, Stevens argued that the South's conduct during the war justified a thorough and all-encompassing plan of Reconstruction — "a radical reorganization in Southern institutions, habits and manners." The United States still held the states of the former Confederacy in the grasp of war, justifying a forceful and activist Recon-struction. From Stevens's perspective, no punishment was too severe for the southern slaveholding elite that had led the nation to war. If this class remained in power, four years of horrific bloodshed would be for naught. At the heart of Stevens's platform was the confiscation and redistribu-tion of land. By taking the property of the South's largest landowners and parceling it out to the poor of both races, Stevens hoped to eradicate the economic legacies of slavery and to build a true democracy in the South. Economic equality, Stevens argued, was the best guarantee of civil and political rights.

[A]ll writers agree that the victor may inflict punishment upon the van-quished enemy, even to the taking of his life, liberty, or the confiscation of all his property; but that this extreme right is never exercised except upon a cruel, barbarous, obstinate, or dangerous foe who has waged an unjust war.

Upon the character of the belligerent, and the justice of the war, and the manner of conducting it, depends our right to take the lives, liberty and property of the belligerent. This war had its origin in treason without

From "Reconstruction: Hon. Thaddeus Stevens on the Great Topic of the Hour," *New York Times*, 10 September 1865, 2.

one spark of justice. It was prosecuted before notice of it, by robbing our forts and armories, and our navy-yards; by stealing our money from the mints and depositories, and by surrend[er]ing our forts and navies by perjurers who had sworn to support the constitution. In its progress our prisoners, by the authority of the government, were slaughtered in cold blood. Ask Fort Pillow and Fort Wagner.[1] Sixty thousand of our prisoners have been deliberately starved to death because they would not enlist in the rebel armies. The graves at Andersonville have each an accusing tongue.[2] The purpose and avowed object of the enemy "to found an empire whose corner-stone should be slavery,"[3] rendered its perpetuity or revival dangerous to human liberty.

Surely, these things are sufficient to justify the exercise of the extreme rights of war — "to execute, to imprison, to confiscate." How many captive enemies it would be proper to execute, as an example to nations, I leave others to judge. I am not fond of sanguinary punishments, but surely some victims must propitiate the manes[4] of our starved, murdered, slaughtered martyrs. A court-martial could do justice according to law.

But we propose to confiscate all the estate of every rebel belligerent whose estate was worth $10,000 or whose land exceeded two hundred acres in quantity. . . .

There are about six millions of freedmen in the South. The number of acres of land is 465,000,000. Of this, those who own above two hundred acres each number about 70,000 persons, holding, in the aggregate, (together with the States,) about 394,000,000 acres, leaving for all the others below 200 each about 71,000,000 of acres. By thus forfeiting the estates of the leading rebels, the government would have 394,000,000 of acres, beside their town property, and yet nine-tenths of the people would remain untouched. Divide this land into convenient farms. Give, if you please, forty acres to each adult male freedman. Suppose there are one million of them. That would require 40,000,000 of acres, which, deducted from 394,000,000, leaves 354,000,000 of acres for sale. Divide it into suitable farms, and sell it to the highest bidders. I think it, includ-

[1] Stevens here refers to two Civil War battles in which Confederate soldiers treated black Union prisoners with particular cruelty.

[2] Andersonville, Georgia, was the site of a Confederate military prison. Its commandant, Henry Wirz, was executed in November 1865, becoming the only Confederate official to suffer this fate.

[3] Stevens is paraphrasing a comment made by Alexander Stephens, vice president of the Confederacy, in 1861. Stephens called slavery the "corner-stone" of the new Confederate nation.

[4] That is, repay the sacrifices.

ing town pro[p]erty, would average at least $10 per acre. That would produce $3,540,000,000—three billions five hundred and forty millions of dollars.

Let that be applied as follows to wit:

1. Invest $300,000,000 in six per cent government bonds, and add the interest semi-annually to the pensions of those who have become entitled by this villainous war.

2. Appropriate $200,000,000 to pay the damages done to loyal men, North and South, by the rebellion.

3. Pay the residue, being $3,040,000,000 towards the payment of the National debt. . . .

But it is said, by those who have more sympathy with rebel wives and children than for the widows and orphans of loyal men, that this stripping the rebels of their estates and driving them to exile or to honest labor, would be harsh and severe upon the innocent women and children. It may be so; but that is the result of the necessary laws of war. But it is revolutionary, say they. This plan would, no doubt, work a radical reorganization in Southern institutions, habits and manners. It is intended to revolutionize their principles and feelings. This may startle feeble minds and shake weak nerves. So do all great improvements in the political and moral world. It requires a heavy impetus to drive forward a sluggish people. When it was first proposed to free the slaves and arm the blacks, did not the nation tremble? The prim conservatives, the snobs, and the male waiting-maids in Congress, were in hysterics.

The whole fabric of Southern society must be changed, and never can it be done if this opportunity is lost. Without this, this government can never be, as it has never been, a true republic. Heretofore, it had more the features of aristocracy than of democracy. The Southern States have been despotisms, not governments of the people. It is impossible that any practical equality of rights can exist where a few thousand men monopolize the whole landed property. The larger the number of small proprietors the more safe and stable the government. . . . How can republican institutions, free schools, free churches, free social intercourse, exist in a mingled community of nabobs and serfs; of the owners of twenty thousand acre manors with lordly palaces, and the occupants of narrow huts inhabited by "low white trash"? If the South is ever to be made a safe republic, let her lands be cultivated by the toils of the owners, or the free labor of intelligent citizens. This must be done, even though it drive her nobility into exile. If they go, all the better.

9

GEORGE W. JULIAN

Speech on the "Grasp of War" Doctrine
November 17, 1865

George W. Julian, representative from Indiana, was one of the most consistently Radical voices in Congress. In this speech, delivered before the Indiana state House of Representatives in Indianapolis, Julian warned against undue leniency in dealing with the defeated Confederacy. With bitter sarcasm, Julian mocked the policies of President Johnson and his supporters. In Julian's view, Johnson's charity amounted to a betrayal of the Union soldiers who had died in the struggle against the Confederacy. In making his case, Julian relied on the "grasp of war" doctrine. Instead of a hasty restoration of full political rights, he insisted that the former Confederacy deserved to be treated as a conquered foe. Having made war on the nation and lost, the South had no rights and could make no demands. To welcome the defeated region back into the nation without first securing guarantees against future hostility and aggression seemed to Julian the height of foolishness. He urged loyal Republicans to demand a true Reconstruction of the South so that the sacrifices of the Civil War would not be in vain.

Now, the law of nations declares that the rights of a conquered people are exactly such rights as the conqueror may graciously be pleased to grant. That is all, gentlemen, and I am for giving the rebels the full benefit of it. When they waged a public war against the nation, went outside the Constitution and defied its power, and rested their cause on the naked ground of lawless might; and when we at last met them on their own chosen issue and flogged them, they had no rights left. Uncle Samuel had them on their backs in the gutter, with his big foot on their necks, and unless by his grace and pleasure they had no longer any right but to die. . . . State rights, constitutional rights, civil rights, natural rights, all the rights there are, were swallowed up and lost by

From George W. Julian, *Speeches on Political Questions* (New York: Hurd and Houghton, 1872), 289–90.

their infernal treason and war. . . . The way is perfectly open to you, unobstructed by any constitutional difficulty, any obstacle in any form, to do exactly what may seem right in your eyes. You can hold the rebels in the strong grasp of war till the end and purpose of the war, which is a lasting peace, shall be made sure. Are any of you silly enough to grant that after they have waged a frightful war of four years on the pretext of State Rights, and we have conquered them, at great cost of blood and money and wide-spread sorrow in the land, we must allow them in the end to set up State Rights again as a bar to our doing precisely what we please? Did we fight them as a mighty public foe, guided by the rules of war and the law of nations up to the moment of the surrender of General Lee, and then, by some devilish necromancy, were we forced to make a dead halt, and recognize in them the very rights they had sinned away? That doctrine is excellent for Copperheads,[1] but in the name of decency, let no Republican mouth it. God forbid! If an assassin assail me, and after a fearful struggle I prostrate him, and wrest from him his weapons, shall I let him up, restore to him his knife and revolver, and politely ask him about terms of peace? Gentlemen, I pray you not to forget the cost of this war. In considering the terms and conditions of peace, do not forget the rivers of blood and seas of fire through which so many of our brave legions waded to their death. Do not, I beseech you, so soon forget the widows and orphans made to mourn through stricken lives to their graves, and the green mounds under which sleep so much of the glory, and pride, and beauty of our Israel.[2] And will you remember all this, and then turn to the rebels as "misguided fellow-citizens," "erring brethren," "wayward sisters," and ask them about the conditions of peace? Shall we tell them that our conquest over them, in-stead of stripping them of their rights, only restores those rights? — that we fought for a military victory, utterly barren of any other results, and that the States to-day in revolt are in the Union, with all their rights in-hering, state and constitutional, and have never been out? Shall we deal with conquered traitors and public enemies as equal sovereigns with ourselves, and insult justice and mock God by pettifogging their cause? Gentlemen, I repeat it, the rebels are in our power, and if we foolishly surrender it we shall be the most recreant people on earth. The glori-ous fruits of our victory are within our grasp. We have only to reach

---

[1] "Copperhead" was derogatory Republican slang for northern Democrats.

[2] Julian does not refer here to the modern nation of Israel, which did not exist in 1865. Instead, he connects the experience of the United States to that of the biblical Israelites.

forth our hands to possess them. Let me plead with you to do your duty. Breathe into the hearts of your rulers your own spirit of earnestness and resolution. Compass this administration about with that persistent pressure which at last gave the country a saving policy of the war under Mr. Lincoln. Do not shrink from the duty of frank and friendly criticism of the conduct of your public servants, when you see them in danger of going astray. Thunder it in the ears of your President and Congress that you demand the hanging, certainly the exile, of the great rebel leaders; the confiscation and distribution of their great landed estates; and that the governing power in the South shall be placed in the hands of the friends, and not the enemies of the nation. Do this, and the result will be a peace with the South as lasting as her hills, and our Republic will be in reality, for the first time in her history, the model Republic of the world.

10

THOMAS NAST

"Pardon" and "Franchise"

August 5, 1865

Thomas Nast's cartoons, published in Harper's Weekly, *offer an important perspective on the politics of the post–Civil War era. Nast was a loyal supporter of the Republican party throughout the period. In his cartoons, Nast displayed a clear opposition to Andrew Johnson and his policies. He regularly depicted the violence and disloyalty of the white South, and during the early part of Reconstruction he was largely sympathetic to southern African Americans. Later Nast images, however, freely perpetuated damaging racial stereotypes. The images shown here, titled "Pardon" and "Franchise," appeared together in an August 1865 issue of* Harper's Weekly. *As a pair, these images juxtaposed the citizenship claims of former Confederates with that of a black Union veteran. In so doing, they criticized Andrew Johnson's lenient Reconstruction policy while making the case for black suffrage.*

PARDON.

COLUMBIA.—"SHALL I TRUST THESE MEN,

From *Harper's Weekly*, 5 August 1865, Nast, Thomas (1840–1902)/Minneapolis Institute of Arts, Minn., USA/Gift of Charlotte Karlen/Bridgeman Images.

From *Harper's Weekly*, 5 August 1865, Nast, Thomas (1840–1902) / Minneapolis Institute of Arts, Minn., USA / Gift of Charlotte Karlen / Bridgeman Images.

FRANCHISE.
AND NOT THIS MAN?"

11

Northern Voters Reject Black Suffrage
1865

Even as Radical Republicans called for black suffrage in the former Confederacy, northern voters proved unwilling to extend the franchise to African Americans in their home states. During the fall of 1865, three northern states — Wisconsin, Minnesota, and Connecticut — placed black suffrage initiatives on their ballots. In all three states, the measures failed to pass. In this article, the New York Times, a moderate Republican newspaper, reported on the defeat of black suffrage in Connecticut. It expressed regret over the outcome but sympathized with the feelings of northern voters unprepared for further shifts in the nation's racial landscape. In its last paragraph, the article claimed that the Radical Republicans and their allies had alienated the northern public with their "ultra devotion to the negro." The failure of the Connecticut suffrage referendum highlights the stubborn persistence of racial prejudice, North as well as South.

The people of Connecticut have decided by about 5,000 majority, that they will not permit negroes to vote. They are to be excluded from suffrage, not because they lack intelligence or capacity, but solely and simply because they are black. . . .

The decision is purely due to *prejudice* — an unreasonable, unjust and cruel prejudice — against the negro. . . . Almost every just and right-minded man will concede that on grounds of pure reason, other things being equal, a black man and a white man should hold exactly the same relations to society and the State, enjoy equal advantage, exercise the same powers, and be protected in the same rights. Some may be prepared and willing to act upon this conviction, and to admit the negro in all respects to precisely that equality. But there will always be a great many others who will not. "Blood is thicker than water," and differences of race, so broad and so strongly marked as those which separate whites and blacks, will make themselves permanently and decisively felt upon political and social relations. . . .

"The Connecticut Election," *New York Times*, 4 October 1865, 4.

The negro is now free, just as free, in the eye of the government and the law, as the white. He suffers still under some disabilities, personal, social and political; but none that can for a moment be compared with the gigantic wrong from which he has just been delivered at such a vast expense of the nation's life and treasure. Appeals on his behalf have thus lost half the force which slavery gave them. The nation has done so much for the negro and at such a cost, that it does not feel called upon just now to do much more.

Besides, there can be no doubt that the country is tired and disgusted with the extreme and extravagant style in which the claims of the negro have been pressed. By a very active and peremptory school of political and social reformers, the claims, interests, courage and character of the whites have been made wholly subordinate to those of the blacks. There must in the nature of things be a reaction to all this—and the Connecticut election indicates that it has begun. How far it will go, or what results it will accomplish, remains to be seen. It will probably, at all events, somewhat dampen the ardor of ambitious politicians who have supposed ultra devotion to the negro the only winning card, and it may possibly satisfy party leaders that it is not always safe rashly to insert new planks in a party platform.

12

MISSISSIPPI LEGISLATURE

Acts Relating to the Freedpeople

1865

The southern state legislatures convened under Presidential Recon-struction quickly proved Radical fears warranted. In their first postwar session, the legislature of Mississippi passed a number of acts designed to control the behavior of formerly enslaved African Americans. Other south-ern states soon passed similar "Black Codes." Though some provisions extended legal protections to African Americans—including the right to contract, the right to testify in court, and the right to marry—most

From Edward McPherson, *The Political History of the United States of America during the Period of Reconstruction* (Washington, D.C.: Philp & Solomons, 1871), 29–32.

sought to ensure that the freedpeople remained a subordinate class bound to plantation labor. The Black Codes curtailed civil liberties, limited employment opportunities, and denied freedom of movement. In Mississippi, legislators established an apprenticeship system that forced black minors to work for their former masters. They also required all African Americans to demonstrate written evidence of employment each January or face criminal prosecution. Other provisions prevented gun ownership by blacks, barred the sale of alcohol, and placed limits on freedom of speech and assembly. For northern Radical Republicans, the Black Codes provided undeniable evidence that Presidential Reconstruction was a failure, and proof that southern whites were incapable of dealing justly with the freedpeople.

An Act to regulate the Relation of Master and Apprentice relative to Freedmen, Free Negroes, and Mulattoes, November 22, 1865

SEC. 1 provides that it shall be the duty of all sheriffs, justices of the peace, and other civil officers of the several counties in this State to report to the probate courts of their respective counties semi-annually, at the January and July terms of said courts, all freedmen, free negroes, and mulattoes, under the age of eighteen, within their respective counties, beats, or districts, who are orphans, or whose parent or parents have not the means, or who refuse to provide for and support said minors, and thereupon it shall be the duty of said probate court to order the clerk of said court to apprentice said minors to some competent and suitable person, on such terms as the court may direct, having a particular care to the interest of said minors: *Provided,* That the former owner of said minors shall have the preference when, in the opinion of the court, he or she shall be a suitable person for that purpose. . . .

SEC. 3 provides that in the management and control of said apprentices said master or mistress shall have power to inflict such moderate corporeal chastisement as a father or guardian is allowed to inflict on his or her child or ward at common law: *Provided,* That in no case shall cruel or inhuman punishment be inflicted. . . .

The Vagrant Act, November 24, 1865

. . . SEC. 2 provides that all freedmen, free negroes, and mulattoes in this State, over the age of eighteen years, found on the second Monday in January, 1866, or thereafter, with no lawful employment or business, or found unlawfully assembling themselves together, either in the day or night time, and all white persons so assembling with freedmen, free negroes, or mulattoes, or usually associating with freedmen, free negroes, or mulattoes on terms of equality, or living in adultery or fornication with a freedwoman, free negro, or mulatto, shall be deemed vagrants, and on conviction thereof shall be fined in the sum of not exceeding, in the case of a freedman, free negro or mulatto, fifty dollars, and a white man two hundred dollars, and imprisoned, at the discretion of the court, the free negro not exceeding ten days, and the white man not exceeding six months. . . .

An Act to confer Civil Rights on Freedmen, and for other Purposes, November 25, 1865

. . . Sec. 3 further provides that all freedmen, free negroes and mulattoes, who do now and have heretofore lived and cohabited together as husband and wife[,] shall be taken and held in law as legally married, and the issue shall be taken and held legitimate as for all purposes. That it shall not be lawful for any freedman, free negro or mulatto to intermarry with any white person; nor for any white person to intermarry with any freedman, free negro or mulatto; and any person who shall so intermarry shall be deemed guilty of felony, and on conviction thereof, shall be confined in the State penitentiary for life. . . .

Sec. 5 provides that every freedman, free negro, and mulatto shall on the second Monday of January, one thousand eight hundred and sixty-six, and annually thereafter, have a lawful home or employment, and shall have written evidence thereof. . . .

Sec. 7 provides that every civil officer shall, and every person may arrest and carry back to his or her legal employer any freedman, free negro, or mulatto who shall have quit the service of his or her employer before the expiration of his or her term of service without good cause; and said officer and person shall be entitled to receive for arresting and carrying back every deserting employé aforesaid the sum of five dollars, and ten cents per mile from the place of arrest to the place of delivery, and the same shall be paid by the employer and held as a set-off for so much against the wages of said deserting employé. . . .

Sec. 9 provides that if any person shall persuade, or attempt to persuade, entice, or cause any freedman, free negro, or mulatto to desert from the legal employment of any person before the expiration of his or her term of service, or shall knowingly employ any such deserting freedman, free negro, or mulatto, or shall knowingly give or sell to any such deserting freedman, free negro, or mulatto any food, raiment, or other thing, he or she shall be guilty of a misdemeanor, and upon conviction shall be fined not less than twenty-five dollars and not more than two hundred dollars. . . .

An Act to punish certain Offences therein named, and for other purposes, November 29, 1865

SEC. 1. *Be it enacted &c.*, That no freedman, free negro, or mulatto, not in the military service of the United States Government, and not licensed to do so by the board of police of his or her county, shall keep or carry fire-arms of any kind, or any ammunition, dirk,[1] or bowie-knife; and on conviction thereof, in the county court, shall be punished by fine, not exceeding ten dollars. . . .

SEC. 2. That any freedman, free negro, or mulatto, committing riots, routes, affrays, trespasses, malicious mischief and cruel treatment to animals, seditious speeches, insulting gestures, language, or acts, or assaults on any person, disturbance of the peace, exercising the functions of a minister of the gospel without a license from some regularly organized church, vending spirituous or intoxicating liquors, or committing any other misdemeanor, the punishment of which is not specifically provided for by law, shall, upon conviction thereof, in the county court, be fined not less than ten dollars, and not more than one hundred dollars, and may be imprisoned, at the discretion of the court, not exceeding thirty days. . . .

SEC. 5. That if any freedman, free negro or mulatto, convicted of any of the misdemeanors provided against in this act, shall fail or refuse, for the space of five days after conviction, to pay the fine and costs imposed, such person shall be hired out by the sheriff or other officer, at public outcry, to any white person who will pay said fine and all costs, and take such convict for the shortest time.

[1] A type of dagger.

13

ELIZABETH CADY STANTON

Letter in Support of Women's Suffrage
December 26, 1865

For much of the late antebellum period, the antislavery and women's rights movements were closely aligned. In the wake of the Civil War, however, the interests and agendas of the two began to diverge. In the early months of Reconstruction, abolitionist Wendell Phillips had asked feminist reformers to exercise patience, claiming "this hour belongs to the negro." In this letter to Phillips, published in the National Anti-Slavery Standard, *women's rights advocate Elizabeth Cady Stanton urged the nation to embrace full, unfettered democracy. Such an opportunity was not likely to present itself again, she argued. If the Constitution was to be amended, women should be enfranchised along with African Americans. Though Stanton's intention was not to suggest that black men were less deserving of the vote than white women—she demanded the ballot for both—some of her comments certainly imply such an unfavorable comparison. Her description of "degraded, ignorant" black men suggests the limits of the interracial reform alliance that had tied women's rights to abolitionism.*

By an amendment of the Constitution, ratified by three-fourths of the loyal states, the black man is declared free. The largest and most influential party is demanding suffrage for him throughout the union, which right in many states is already conceded. Although this may remain for five or ten years a question for politicians to wrangle over, the black man is now, from a political point of view, far above the educated women of the country. For the last thirty years the representative women of the nation have done their uttermost to secure freedom for the negro, and so long as he was lowest in the scale of being we were willing to press his claims. We are asking ourselves whether it would not be wiser

From Theodore Stanton and Harriet Stanton Blatch, eds., *Elizabeth Cady Stanton as Revealed in Her Letters, Diary, and Reminiscences*, Vol. 2 (New York: Harper & Brothers Publishers, 1922), 109–11.

when the constitutional door is open, to push in by the negro's side, and thus make the gap so wide that no privileged class could ever again close it against the humblest citizen of the Republic. You say, "This is the negro's hour." I will not insist that there are women of that race, but ask, Is there not danger that he, once intrenched [*sic*] in all his inalienable rights, may be an added power to hold us at bay? Why should the African prove more just and generous than his Saxon compeers? Again, if the two millions of southern black women are not to be secured in their rights of person, property, wages, and children, then their emancipation is but another form of slavery. In fact, it is better to be the slave of an educated white man, than that of a degraded, ignorant black one. We who know what absolute power is given to man, in all his civil, political, and social relations, by the statute laws of most of the states, demand that in changing the status of the four millions of Africans, the women as well as the men shall be secured in all the rights, privileges, and immunities of citizens. If our prayer involved a new set of measures, or a new train of thought, it might be cruel to tax white male citizens with even two simple questions at a time. But the disfranchised all make the same demand, and the same logic and justice which secures suffrage for one class gives it to all. . . . Now is our opportunity to retrieve the errors of the past and mould anew the elements of democracy. The nation is ready for a long step in the right direction. Party lines are obliterated, and all men are thinking for themselves. If our rulers have the justice to give the black man suffrage, woman should avail herself of this new-born virtue and secure her rights. If not, she should begin with renewed earnestness to educate the people into the idea of true universal suffrage.

2

Defending Civil Rights

14

ANDREW JOHNSON

First Annual Message

December 4, 1865

By the time the Congress reconvened in early December 1865, six full months had passed since Andrew Johnson's May Proclamations set the course for Presidential Reconstruction. In his annual message for the year 1865, Johnson surveyed the progress made toward the "restoration" of the South. Because he believed that secession was legally impossible, Johnson argued that the states of the South had never actually left the Union. As such, he believed they should be returned to full political participation as quickly as possible. By December 1865, the southern states had rewritten their constitutions, established new state governments, and sent senators and representatives to Washington, D.C. Thus, Johnson considered the Reconstruction process to be largely complete.

Though Johnson encouraged the southern states to ratify the Thirteenth Amendment as an act of goodwill, he anticipated no further federal intervention on behalf of southern African Americans. Ignoring widespread reports of anti-black violence and the obviously discriminatory intentions of the Black Codes, Johnson urged Congress to adopt a hands-off policy with regard to the freedpeople, leaving southern whites to manage the transition to freedom.

From James D. Richardson, ed., *A Compilation of the Messages and Papers of the Presidents, 1789–1908*, Vol. VI (n.p.: Bureau of National Literature and Art, 1909), 356–61.

It has been my steadfast object to escape from the sway of momentary passions and to derive a healing policy from the fundamental and unchanging principles of the Constitution.

I found the States suffering from the effects of a civil war. Resistance to the General Government appeared to have exhausted itself. The United States had recovered possession of their forts and arsenals, and their armies were in the occupation of every State which had attempted to secede. Whether the territory within the limits of those States should be held as conquered territory, under military authority emanating from the President as the head of the Army, was the first question that presented itself for decision. . . .

[T]he policy of military rule over a conquered territory would have implied that the States whose inhabitants may have taken part in the rebellion had by the act of those inhabitants ceased to exist. But the true theory is that all pretended acts of secession were from the beginning null and void. The States can not commit treason nor screen the individual citizens who may have committed treason any more than they can make valid treaties or engage in lawful commerce with any foreign power. The States attempting to secede placed themselves in a condition where their vitality was impaired, but not extinguished; their functions suspended, but not destroyed.

But if any State neglects or refuses to perform its offices there is more need that the General Government should maintain all its authority and as soon as practicable resume the exercise of all its functions. On this principle I have acted, and have gradually and quietly, and by almost imperceptible steps, sought to restore the rightful energy of the General Government and of the States. To that end provisional governors have been appointed for the States, conventions called, governors elected, legislatures assembled, and Senators and Representatives chosen to the Congress of the United States. . . . And is it not happy for us all that the restoration of each one of these functions of the General Government brings with it a blessing to the States over which they are extended? Is it not a sure promise of harmony and renewed attachment to the Union that after all that has happened the return of the General Government is known only as a beneficence? . . .

The next step which I have taken to restore the constitutional relations of the States has been an invitation to them to participate in the high office of amending the Constitution. Every patriot must wish for a general amnesty at the earliest epoch consistent with public safety. For this great end there is need of concurrence of all opinions and the spirit of mutual conciliation. All parties in the late terrible conflict must work together in harmony. It is not too much to ask, in the name of the whole people, that on the one side the plan of restoration shall proceed in conformity with a willingness to cast the disorders of the past into oblivion, and that on the other the evidence of sincerity in the future maintenance of the Union shall be put beyond any doubt by the ratification of the proposed amendment to the Constitution, which provides for the abolition of slavery forever within the limits of our country. So long as the adoption of this amendment is delayed, so long will doubt and jealousy and uncertainty prevail. . . .

The amendment to the Constitution being adopted, it would remain for the States whose powers have been so long in abeyance to resume their places in the two branches of the National Legislature, and thereby complete the work of restoration. Here it is for you, fellow-citizens of the Senate, and for you, fellow-citizens of the House of Representatives, to judge, each of you for yourselves, of the elections, returns, and qualifications of your own members. . . .

The relations of the General Government toward the 4,000,000 inhabitants whom the war has called into freedom have engaged my most serious consideration. . . .

In my judgment the freedmen, if they show patience and manly virtues, will sooner obtain a participation in the elective franchise through the States than through the General Government, even if it had power to intervene. When the tumult of emotions that have been raised by the suddenness of the social change shall have subsided, it may prove that they will receive the kindest usage from some of those on whom they have heretofore most closely depended. . . .

I know that sincere philanthropy is earnest for the immediate realization of its remotest aims; but time is always an element in reform. It is one of the greatest acts on record to have brought 4,000,000 people into freedom. The career of free industry must be fairly opened to them, and then their future prosperity and condition must, after all, rest mainly on themselves.

15

CHARLES SUMNER

Speech on the "Actual Condition of the Rebel States"
December 20, 1865

Congressional Republicans disagreed with Johnson's rosy appraisal of southern affairs. When the House and Senate reconvened in early December, they refused to seat the would-be congressmen sent from the southern states. Their actions sent a clear message: The South was neither restored nor reconstructed; the process of Reconstruction was ongoing.

Early in the session, Massachusetts senator Charles Sumner treated his colleagues to an extended speech dedicated to the "actual condition of the Rebel States." Drawing evidence from correspondents all across the South, Sumner documented the white South's continued hostility toward the federal government and offered dozens of examples of white-on-black racial violence. Sumner's depiction of the South — bloody, resentful, rebellious — stood in sharp contrast to that which Johnson had presented in his annual report. Sumner demanded that his colleagues take immediate action to defend the lives and rights of the formerly enslaved. Only Congress had the power to end the bloodshed and protect the freedpeople of the South.

[I]t is my duty to expose the actual condition of the Rebel States, especially as regards loyalty and the treatment of the freedmen. On this head I shall adduce evidence in my possession. In the endeavor to bring what I say within reasonable proportions, I shall adduce only a small part of what has passed under my eye; but it will be more than enough. In bringing it forward, the difficulty is of selection and abridgment. . . .

For instance, a trustworthy traveller, who has recently traversed the Gulf States, thus writes in a private letter to myself: —

"The former masters exhibit a most cruel, remorseless, and vindictive spirit toward the colored people. In parts where there are no Union soldiers I saw colored women treated in the most outrageous manner.

From *The Works of Charles Sumner,* Vol. X (Boston: Lee and Shepard, 1876), 63, 67, 72, 79, 82–83, 96.

They have no rights that are respected. They are killed, and their bodies thrown into ponds or mud-holes. They are mutilated by having ears and noses cut off." . . .

A loyal resident of North Carolina writes me: —

"I tell you, Sir, the only difference now and one year ago is, that the flag is acknowledged as supreme, and there is some fear manifested, and they have no arms. The sentiment is the same. If anything otherwise, more hatred exists toward the Government. *I know there is more toward Union men, both black and white.*" . . .

Where such a spirit prevails, the freedmen fare badly. In Georgia they are treated cruelly. A traveller writes: —

"The hatred toward the negro as a freeman is intense among the low and brutal, who are the vast majority. Murders, shootings, whippings, robbing, and brutal treatment of every kind are daily inflicted upon them, and I am sorry to say in most cases they can get no redress." . . .

It seems that in Georgia there is a body of men known as "Regulators," who are thus described by a correspondent of that journal which has for years whitewashed the enormities of Slavery, the "New York Herald": —

"Springing naturally out of this disordered state of affairs is an organization of 'Regulators,' so called. Their numbers include many ex-Confederate cavaliers of the country, and their mission is to visit summary justice upon any offenders against the public peace. It is needless to say that their attention is largely directed to maintain quiet and submission among the blacks. *The shooting or stringing up of some obstreperous 'nigger' by the 'Regulators' is so common an occurrence as to excite little remark. Nor is the work of proscription confined to the freedmen only.* The 'Regulators' go to the bottom of the matter, and strive to make it uncomfortably warm for any new settler with demoralizing innovations of wages for 'niggers.'"

Such is the unimaginable atrocity which, according to friendly authority, prevails in Georgia. The poor freedman is sacrificed. The Northern settler, believing in Human Rights, is sacrificed also. Alas that such scenes should disgrace our country and age! Alas that there should be hesitation in applying the necessary remedy!

Surely this is enough. I do not stop to dwell on instances of frightful barbarism. One is authenticated in the court of the provost-marshal, where a colored girl was roasted alive! And another writer, in a letter just received, describes a system of "burning" in Wilkes County, Georgia, as "a mild means of extorting from the freed people a confession as to where they have their arms and money concealed." He says, "They were held in the blaze." Think of it, Sir, here, in this Republic, they are held in a blaze! And the National Government looks on! . . .

I bring this plain story to a close. I regret that I have been constrained to present it. I wish it were otherwise. But I should fail in duty, did I fail to speak. Not in anger, not in vengeance, not in harshness, have I spoken, but solemnly, carefully, for the sake of my country and humanity, that peace and reconciliation may again prevail. I have spoken especially for the loyal citizens now trodden down by Rebel power, and without representation on this floor. Would that my voice could help them to security and justice! I can only state the case. It is for you to decide. It is for you to determine how long these things shall continue to shock mankind. You have before you the actual condition of the Rebel region. You have heard the terrible testimony. The blood curdles at the thought of such enormities, and especially at the thought that the poor freedmen, to whom we owe protection, are left to the unrestrained will of such a people, smarting with defeat, and ready to wreak vengeance upon these representatives of a true loyalty. In the name of God, let us protect them.

16

BENJAMIN WADE

Speech on the "Great Principle of Eternal Justice"
January 18, 1866

Benjamin Wade of Ohio was a committed Radical who had served in the Senate since 1851. In this speech, Wade summed up his political creed, explaining that the principle of "eternal justice" had guided him throughout his long career. Describing his years as an abolitionist in a largely proslavery Senate, Wade argued that the battle against slavery would not be won until equal rights had been secured for African Americans. The principle of eternal justice demanded that Wade settle for nothing less than complete racial equality.

From Cong. Globe, 39th Cong., 1st Sess., 293.

Significantly, Wade praised Andrew Johnson for his staunch refusal to equivocate on the abolition of slavery. He insisted, however, that emancipation was not enough. Without a guarantee of equality before the law, African American lives and livelihoods remained insecure. Responding to imperatives both personal and political, Wade saw in Reconstruction an opportunity to complete his life's work.

In the counsels that I have given and the measures that I have advocated in the Senate, I have ever had one polar star to guide my action, and to that I adhere whether I am in the majority or the minority, and I never intend to be tempted from it one single inch. I fix my eye upon the great principle of eternal justice, and it has borne me triumphantly through all difficulties in my legislative career since I have had a seat here. I say triumphantly, for, sir, I have stood upon this floor when I had not ten men to support me against the entire Senate, and when the principles that I advocated were infinitely more unpopular here than those that I announce to-day. How were the whole Senate startled at the idea of universal emancipation fifteen years ago, ten years ago; yes, sir, five years ago! Talk not to me about unpopular doctrines, and endeavor not to intimidate me by the intimation that I shall be found in a minority among the people! I know them better. I think I know that I tread in the great path of rectitude and right, and I care not who opposes me. God Almighty is my guide: He, going before to strengthen my hand, has never failed me yet, and I do not fear that He will do so on this occasion. . . .

I wish, sir, and I wish nothing more heartily, that I could agree exactly with the President's view of the subject and go along with him in the smooth path to a final and speedy adjustment of this whole question; but there are things in that path which prevent my seeing the way clearly. I give the President full credit for all that he has done, and I honor him for the pertinacious manner in which he has insisted on the great guarantees to which I have already alluded. He has commenced, as it were, to build this great arch of freedom aright; he has laid the foundations deep upon the rock of justice and truth; he has demanded that slavery be abolished. I agree with him in this, and I honor him because he has stood firmly by this demand, and he stands firmly by it now. All these requisitions that he has demanded of the South are right, but he has failed to put the keystone on the arch that he has built, and if you leave it as it is it will go to ruin.

When this great question is settled, I want it to be finally and entirely disposed of. I do not wish to be fighting eternally about slavery and distinctions of rights and privileges among the American people. I say to President Johnson, to the Democratic party, to the people of the United States, that I will never yield this controversy until all men in America shall stand precisely upon the same platform, equal before the law in every respect. When that shall have been secured, I shall give up this great controversy in which I have been engaged so many years, and no man will be more rejoiced than myself that I shall be relieved from it.

17

LYMAN TRUMBULL

Speech on the Civil Rights Bill
January 29, 1866

By the time Congress assembled in December 1865, most congressional Republicans agreed that Andrew Johnson's lenient Reconstruction policies had proven insufficient. The question was how to proceed. Although Radicals advanced a number of plans, Congress initially adopted a relatively moderate course.

Lyman Trumbull of Illinois was one of the most significant moderate Republican voices in the Senate. In the early months of 1866, Trumbull brought forward two important pieces of Reconstruction legislation. The first was a bill to extend the life of the Freedmen's Bureau, a federal organization chartered during the war to aid the formerly enslaved in their transition to freedom. The second piece of legislation, the Civil Rights Bill, expanded the basis of citizenship to include African Americans and enumerated the civil rights owed to all citizens, regardless of race.

In this speech in the Senate, Trumbull explained the need for a Civil Rights Bill with direct reference to the Black Codes passed by southern legislatures. The Thirteenth Amendment had provided freedom, he explained, but the Civil Rights Bill was needed to secure "practical freedom." As it expanded the bounds of citizenship, the Civil Rights Bill

From Cong. Globe, 39th Cong., 1st Sess., 474–76.

*established a basic equality of legal rights as the birthright of all Ameri-
can citizens. Trumbull's bill was thus an attempt to complete the work of
emancipation. As it outlawed discriminatory legislation like the Black
Codes, the bill would give real meaning to the abstract concept of freedom.*

I regard the bill to which the attention of the Senate is now called as the
most important measure that has been under its consideration since
the adoption of the constitutional amendment abolishing slavery. That
amendment declared that all persons in the United States should be
free. This measure is intended to give effect to that declaration and secure to all persons within the United States practical freedom. There is
very little importance in the general declaration of abstract truths and
principles unless they can be carried into effect, unless the persons who
are to be affected by them have some means of availing themselves of
their benefits. Of what avail was the immortal declaration "that all men
are created equal; that they are endowed by their Creator with certain
inalienable rights; that among these are life, liberty, and the pursuit of
happiness," and "that to secure these rights Governments are instituted
among men," to the millions of the African race in this country who
were ground down and degraded and subjected to a slavery more intol-
erable and cruel than the world ever before knew? . . .

Since the abolition of slavery, the Legislatures which have assembled
in the insurrectionary States have passed laws relating to the freedmen,
and in nearly all the States they have discriminated against them. They
deny them certain rights, subject them to severe penalties, and still
impose upon them the very restrictions which were imposed upon them
in consequence of the existence of slavery, and before it was abolished.
The purpose of the bill under consideration is to destroy all these dis-
criminations, and to carry into effect the constitutional amendment. . . .

I take it that any statute which is not equal to all, and which deprives
any citizen of civil rights which are secured to other citizens, is an unjust
encroachment upon his liberty; and is, in fact, a badge of servitude
which, by the Constitution, is prohibited. . . .

In my judgment, persons of African descent, born in the United
States, are as much citizens as white persons who are born in the
country. I know that in the slaveholding States a different opinion has
obtained. The people of those States have not regarded the colored race
as citizens, and on that principle many of their laws making discrimina-
tions between the whites and the colored people are based; but it is

competent for Congress to declare, under the Constitution of the United States, who are citizens. If there were any question about it, it would be settled by the passage of a law declaring all persons born in the United States to be citizens thereof. That this bill proposes to do. Then they will be entitled to the rights of citizens. And what are they? The great fundamental rights set forth in this bill: the right to acquire property, the right to go and come at pleasure, the right to enforce rights in the courts, to make contracts, and to inherit and dispose of property. These are the very rights that are set forth in this bill as appertaining to every freeman. . . .

With this bill passed into a law and efficiently executed we shall have secured freedom in fact and equality in civil rights to all persons in the United States.

18

Black Delegation to the White House Calls for Civil and Political Rights
February 7, 1866

On February 7, 1866, an African American delegation visited the White House to meet with President Johnson. The delegation included Frederick Douglass, the nation's leading black orator, and George T. Downing, a business owner and political activist, who presented the opening statement reprinted here. On its own, Downing insisted, emancipation was insufficient. He therefore called for full civil and political rights for African Americans throughout the nation. In a lengthy response, Johnson questioned the need for federal protection of African American rights, suggesting that such matters were better left to the states. Johnson's statement sent troubling signals to supporters of black civil rights.

From Edward McPherson, *The Political History of the United States of America during the Period of Reconstruction* (Washington, D.C.: Philp & Solomons, 1871), 52.

We present ourselves to your Excellency, to make known with pleasure the respect which we are glad to cherish for you—a respect which is your due, as our Chief Magistrate. It is our desire for you to know that we come feeling that we are friends meeting a friend. . . . We are in a passage to equality before the law. God hath made it by opening a Red Sea. We would have your assistance through the same. We come to you in the name of the colored people of the United States. We are delegated to come by some who have unjustly worn iron manacles on their bodies—by some whose minds have been manacled by class legislation in the States called free. . . .

Our coming is a marked circumstance, noting determined hope that we are not satisfied with an amendment prohibiting slavery, but that we wish it enforced with appropriate legislation. This is our desire. We ask for it intelligently, with the knowledge and conviction that the fathers of the Revolution intended freedom for every American; that they should be protected in their rights as citizens, and be equal before the law. We are Americans, native born Americans. We are citizens; we are glad to have it known to the world that you bear no doubtful record on this point. On this fact, and with confidence in the triumph of justice, we base our hope. We see no recognition of color or race in the organic law of the land. It knows no privileged class, and therefore we cherish the hope that we may be fully enfranchised, not only here in this District, but throughout the land. We respectfully submit that rendering anything less than this will be rendering to us less than our just due; that granting anything less than our full rights will be a disregard of our just rights and of due respect for our feelings. If the powers that be do so it will be used as a license, as it were, or an apology, for any community, or for individuals thus disposed, to outrage our rights and feelings. It has been shown in the present war that the Government may justly reach its strong arm into States, and demand from them, from those who owe it allegiance, their assistance and support. May it not reach out a like arm to secure and protect its subject upon who[m] it has a claim?

19

The Civil Rights Bill
March 1866

Lyman Trumbull's Civil Rights Bill passed Congress in early March 1866. The Civil Rights Bill made the legal equality of rights a matter of federal law. The heart of the bill was its first section, which defined all persons born in the United States—with the exception of Indians—as U.S. citizens. The first section went on to enumerate the rights that citizenship guaranteed, including the right to make contracts, hold property, sue and testify in court, and enjoy "full and equal benefit" of all state and federal laws. The second section of the bill prescribed penalties for legal discrimination on the basis of skin color, while the third section empowered federal district courts to hear cases relating to the infringement of African American civil rights. Later sections of the Civil Rights Bill dealt with implementation and enforcement.

The Civil Rights Bill, it is important to note, dealt exclusively with the legal equality of citizens. On the issue of political rights—that is, the right to vote—the Civil Rights Bill said nothing. Moderate Republicans like Trumbull were prepared to mobilize the federal government to protect African American civil rights, but the issue of black suffrage remained controversial.

An Act to protect all persons in the United States in their civil rights, and furnish the means of their vindication.

Be it enacted, &c., That all persons born in the United States and not subject to any foreign power, excluding Indians, not taxed, are hereby declared to be citizens of the United States; and such citizens of every race and color, without regard to any previous condition of slavery or involuntary servitude, except as a punishment for crime whereof the party shall have been duly convicted, shall have the same right in every State and Territory in the United States to make and enforce contracts; to sue, be parties, and give evidence; to inherit, purchase, lease, sell, hold, and convey real and personal property; and to full and equal benefits of

From Edward McPherson, *The Political History of the United States of America during the Period of Reconstruction* (Washington, D.C.: Philp & Solomons, 1871), 78–79.

all laws and proceedings for the security of person and property as is enjoyed by white citizens, and shall be subject to like punishment, pains, and penalties, and to none other, any law, statute[,] ordinance, regulation, or custom, to the contrary notwithstanding.

SEC. 2. That any person who, under color of any law, statute, ordinance, regulation, or custom, shall subject, or cause to be subjected, any inhabitant of any State or Territory to the deprivation of any right secured or protected by this act, or to different punishment, pains, or penalties on account of such person having at any time been held in a condition of slavery or involuntary servitude, except as a punishment for crime whereof the party shall have been duly convicted, or by reason of his color or race, than is prescribed for the punishment of white persons, shall be deemed guilty of a misdemeanor, and, on conviction, shall be punished by fine not exceeding one thousand dollars, or imprisonment not exceeding one year, or both, in the discretion of the court.

SEC. 3. That the district courts of the United States, within their respective districts, shall have, exclusively of the courts of the several States, cognizance of all crimes and offences committed against the provisions of this act, and also, concurrently with the circuit courts of the United States, of all causes, civil and criminal, affecting persons who are denied or cannot enforce in the courts or judicial tribunals of the State or locality where they may be any of the rights secured to them by the first section of this act.

20

ANDREW JOHNSON

Veto of the Civil Rights Bill

March 27, 1866

Given the moderation of the Civil Rights Bill, most commentators expected Andrew Johnson to sign it into law. Instead, Johnson vetoed the bill. In his veto message, Johnson explained his opposition with reference to two themes. He argued, first of all, that the Civil Rights Bill offered benefits to African Americans that the federal government did not provide

From Edward McPherson, *The Political History of the United States of America during the Period of Reconstruction* (Washington, D.C.: Philp & Solomons, 1871), 74–75, 78.

to anyone else. Johnson went so far as to claim that the Civil Rights Bill actually discriminated against white people in its attempts to protect black civil rights. Second, Johnson insisted that the Civil Rights Bill heralded a dangerous centralization of powers in the federal government. This centralization, he believed, threatened to overthrow the nation's system of balanced federalism.

Both of Johnson's objections ignored the events that necessitated such a bill in the first place. The Civil Rights Bill was not an example of undue favoritism toward the freedpeople; it was a response to a concerted campaign of racial discrimination at the state level. In passing the Black Codes, the reconstituted state governments of the South had forced the federal government to take steps to protect African American civil rights. As he attempted to defend the state governments erected under his watch, Johnson found it convenient to ignore some of their more objectionable actions.

I regret that the bill which has passed both Houses of Congress, entitled "An act to protect all persons in the United States in their civil rights, and furnish the means of their vindication," contains provisions which I cannot approve, consistently with my sense of duty to the whole people, and my obligations to the Constitution of the United States. I am therefore constrained to return it to the Senate, the house in which it originated, with my objections to its becoming a law. . . .

[T]he grave question presents itself, whether, when eleven of the thirty-six States are unrepresented in Congress at the present time, it is sound policy to make our entire colored population and all other excepted classes citizens of the United States? Four millions of them have just emerged from slavery into freedom. Can it be reasonably supposed that they possess the requisite qualifications to entitle them to all the privileges and immunities of citizens of the United States? . . . Besides, the policy of the Government, from its origin to the present time, seems to have been that persons who are strangers to and unfamiliar with our institutions and our laws should pass through a certain probation, at the end of which, before attaining the coveted prize, they must give evidence of their fitness to receive and to exercise the rights of citizens, as contemplated by the Constitution of the United States. The bill, in effect, proposes a discrimination against large numbers of intelligent, worthy, and patriotic foreigners, and in favor of the negro, to whom, after long years of bondage, the avenues to freedom and intelligence have just now been suddenly opened. . . .

In all our history, in all our experience as a people, living under federal and State law, no such system as that contemplated by the details of this bill has ever before been proposed or adopted. They establish for the security of the colored race safeguards which go infinitely beyond any that the General Government has ever provided for the white race. In fact, the distinction of race and color is, by the bill, made to operate in favor of the colored and against the white race. They interfere with the municipal legislation of the States, with the relations existing exclusively between a State and its citizens, or between inhabitants of the same State—an absorption and assumption of power by the General Government which, if acquiesced in, must sap and destroy our federative system of limited powers, and break down the barriers which preserve the rights of the States. It is another step, or rather stride, towards centralization, and the concentration of all legislative powers in the national Government. The tendency of the bill must be to resuscitate the spirit of rebellion, and to arrest the progress of those influences which are more closely drawing around the States the bonds of union and peace.

21

HARPER'S WEEKLY

"Outside of the Galleries of the House of Representatives during the Passage of the Civil Rights Bill"

April 28, 1866

Johnson's veto of the Civil Rights Bill unified Republican sentiment in Congress. Both houses quickly mustered the two-thirds majority necessary to pass legislation over a presidential veto. Harper's Weekly, *a popular weekly newsmagazine, commemorated the occasion with this drawing depicting the celebration in the hallways outside the House of Representatives as the deciding votes were cast. The figures depicted in the image on the left—freedpeople and wounded Union veterans—make a strong statement regarding the political and historical significance of the Civil Rights Bill.*

77

22

A Northern Journalist Describes Racial Violence in Memphis, Tennessee

May 1866

In early May 1866, the city of Memphis, Tennessee, erupted in a three-day spasm of racial violence. The incident began as an argument between white city policemen and black Union soldiers, but quickly devolved into a wholesale massacre of African Americans. White mobs roamed the streets of the city, killing black residents, invading homes, and burning buildings. The riot quickly became a national story. The Independent, *a Republican newspaper published in Boston, was appalled at the brutality of white rioters. Denying the accuracy of reports that blamed the violence on African Americans, the paper argued that the events in Memphis offered stark evidence of the failure of Andrew Johnson's lenient Reconstruction policies. Black suffrage, the paper argued, was now the only remedy strong enough to protect the freedpeople from the wrath of their white neighbors.*

It was the lamb that was to blame, in Aesop's time, and before and since, whenever the wolf had a grudge or a greed to gratify at his expense. The weak are always in the wrong, the strong being the judges. . . . The freedmen at Memphis . . . have been hunted in the streets, women and children shot in cold blood, their homes burnt over their heads, and at least one woman burnt alive, their churches and schools burnt to the ground; and it is all their own fault. Some of them are verily guilty of having served in the national army, and it is charged against other miscreants, women as well as men, that they have been seen walking arm and arm in the streets! And all are involved in the general guilt of emancipation. It is no wonder that the righteous indignation of the white population, thus outraged, insulted, and robbed, should seize the first occasion to avenge their wrongs and vindicate the superiority of their race. . . .

That some of the negroes may have exceeded the limits of the calmest and most philosophic patience in the presence of the enemies who sought their lives is not impossible. That they were guilty of defending

"The Memphis Massacre," *The Independent*, 17 May 1866, 4.

themselves to some extent cannot be denied. But that this riot would ever have been begun or carried on by them alone is shown to be absurd by the very statements of the Copperhead press of Memphis. One of these gives an account of the blacks driving the police and the whites generally before them, pouring in volleys of bullets, and being generally victorious at the outset. But the list of the killed and wounded, on either side, as far as obtained, tells a different story. Two white men killed, and six or eight wounded, against at least twenty killed of the blacks, and the usual proportion wounded, shows on which side the numbers and the ferocity were to be found. And then thirty fine houses and eight churches and school-houses burnt shed a hideous light on this shocking page of history, and prevent its being read amiss. . . .

We do not know how President Johnson may regard these exuberances of his fellow-citizens of Tennessee. He may think that such men are fit to be trusted with the protection of the emancipated blacks and with an important share of the government of the whole country. But we apprehend that the great mass of the thinking public at the North will be of the opinion that a moderate probation of such men can not be injurious to the general interests, unless their influence can be counteracted by that of the only class at the South of whose loyalty there can be no question. . . . If these outrages should have the effect of hastening the day when this one guaranty of safety for the negro and the nation shall be secured, it will add another proof of the way in which Providence brings good out of evil to the many which the recent history of the country has afforded.

23

Report of the Joint Select Committee on Reconstruction

June 1866

Shortly after coming into session in December 1865, the two houses of Congress established a joint committee on Reconstruction to explore the state of affairs in the South. The committee's Republican members were evenly divided between the party's Radical and moderate factions. William Pitt Fessenden of Maine, a moderate, chaired the committee. Arch-Radical Thaddeus Stevens was included, but Charles Sumner, considered too extreme, was denied a seat. The committee conducted interviews with leading white southerners, Union army officers, agents of the Freedmen's Bureau, and a handful of southern African Americans. Their findings suggested dire conditions in the South, with violence and disloyalty distressingly common. Furthermore, many informants suggested that Andrew Johnson's policies—particularly his generous amnesty program and his hasty reconstitution of the southern state governments—had encouraged white southern malfeasance.

The Joint Select Committee on Reconstruction submitted its full report in June 1866, concluding that the states of the former Confederacy were not yet entitled to congressional representation. In its report, the committee offered a number of suggestions for further congressional action. Even before the publication of the report, however, Congress had begun work on the committee's most significant recommendation: a Fourteenth Amendment to the Constitution.

When Congress assembled in December last the people of most of the States lately in rebellion had, under the advice of the President, organized local governments, and some of them had acceded to the terms proposed by him. In his annual message he stated, in general terms, what had been done, but he did not see fit to communicate the details for the information of Congress. While in this and in a subsequent message the President urged the speedy restoration of these States, and

From *Report of the Joint Committee on Reconstruction at the First Session Thirty-Ninth Congress* (Washington, D.C.: Government Printing Office, 1866), ix, xiii, xvii–xviii, xxi.

expressed the opinion that their condition was such as to justify their restoration, yet it is quite obvious that Congress must either have acted blindly on that opinion of the President, or proceeded to obtain the information requisite for intelligent action on the subject. . . .

Your committee came to the consideration of the subject referred to them with the most anxious desire to ascertain what was the condition of the people of the States recently in insurrection, and what, if anything, was necessary to be done before restoring them to the full enjoyment of all their original privileges. It was undeniable that the war into which they had plunged the country had materially changed their relations to the people of the loyal States. Slavery had been abolished by constitutional amendment. A large proportion of the population had become, instead of mere chattels, free men and citizens. Through all the past struggle these had remained true and loyal, and had, in large numbers, fought on the side of the Union. It was impossible to abandon them, without securing them their rights as free men and citizens. The whole civilized world would have cried out against such base ingratitude, and the bare idea is offensive to all right-thinking men. Hence it became important to inquire what could be done to secure their rights, civil and political. It was evident to your committee that adequate security could only be found in appropriate constitutional provisions. . . .

The feeling in many portions of the country towards emancipated slaves, especially among the uneducated and ignorant, is one of vindictive and malicious hatred. This deep-seated prejudice against color is assiduously cultivated by the public journals, and leads to acts of cruelty, oppression, and murder, which the local authorities are at no pains to prevent or punish. There is no general disposition to place the colored race, constituting at least two-fifths of the population, upon terms even of civil equality. While many instances may be found where large planters and men of the better class accept the situation, and honestly strive to bring about a better order of things, by employing the freedmen at fair wages and treating them kindly, the general feeling and disposition among all classes are yet totally averse to the toleration of any class of people friendly to the Union, be they white or black; and this aversion is not unfrequently manifested in an insulting and offensive manner. . . .

The evidence of an intense hostility to the federal Union, and an equally intense love of the late confederacy, nurtured by the war, is decisive. While it appears that nearly all are willing to submit, at least for the time being, to the federal authority, it is equally clear that the ruling motive is a desire to obtain the advantages which will be derived from a representation in Congress. Officers of the Union army on duty, and northern men who go south to engage in business, are generally detested and proscribed. Southern men who adhered to the Union are bitterly hated and relentlessly persecuted. In some localities prosecutions have been instituted in State courts against Union officers for acts done in the line of official duty, and similar prosecutions are threatened elsewhere as soon as the United States troops are removed. All such demonstrations show a state of feeling against which it is unmistakably necessary to guard.

The testimony is conclusive that after the collapse of the confederacy the feeling of the people of the rebellious States was that of abject submission. Having appealed to the tribunal of arms, they had no hope except that by the magnanimity of their conquerors their lives, and possibly their property, might be preserved. Unfortunately, the general issue of pardons to persons who had been prominent in the rebellion, and the feeling of kindliness and conciliation manifested by the Executive, and very generally indicated through the northern press, had the effect to render whole communities forgetful of the crime they had committed, defiant towards the federal government, and regardless of their duties as citizens. The conciliatory measures of the government do not seem to have been met even half way. The bitterness and defiance exhibited toward the United States under such circumstances is without a parallel in the history of the world. In return for our leniency we receive only an insulting denial of our authority. In return for our kind desire for the resumption of fraternal relations we receive only an insolent assumption of rights and privileges long since forfeited. The crime we have punished is paraded as a virtue, and the principles of republican government which we have vindicated at so terrible a cost are denounced as unjust and oppressive. . . .

The conclusion of your committee therefore is, that the so-called Confederate States are not, at present, entitled to representation in the Congress of the United States; that, before allowing such representation, adequate security for future peace and safety should be required; that this can only be found in such changes of the organic law as shall determine the civil rights and privileges of all citizens in all parts of the republic, shall place representation on an equitable basis, shall fix a stigma upon treason, and protect the loyal people against future claims for the expenses incurred in support of rebellion and for manumitted slaves, together with an express grant of power in Congress to enforce those provisions. To this end they offer a joint resolution for amending the Constitution of the United States.

24

THADDEUS STEVENS

Speech on the Fourteenth Amendment
June 13, 1866

The Fourteenth Amendment to the Constitution was the result of months of debate and negotiation among House and Senate Republicans. In formulating the amendment, congressional Republicans hoped, first of all, to enshrine black citizenship and civil rights in the Constitution, beyond the reach of shifting majorities and an antagonistic president. Another pressing concern had to do with suffrage. If African Americans were not to be entrusted with the franchise, it was clear that the South should not gain extra seats in Congress on the basis of the abolition of slavery. Some Republicans also hoped to disfranchise former Confederates until the gains of Reconstruction could be secured.

From the perspective of congressional Radicals, the version of the Fourteenth Amendment that passed both houses of Congress in early June was far from perfect. Not only did the amendment fail to enfranchise African Americans, but its second section appeared to give the states permission to limit the suffrage on the grounds of race. A last-minute Senate substitution replaced the third section's disfranchisement of Confederates with a milder provision banning office-holding by Confederates who had previously taken an oath to support the U.S. Constitution.

On the day the House of Representatives was to consider the final version of the Fourteenth Amendment, Thaddeus Stevens gave voice to the Radicals' dilemma. Stevens would vote for the amendment, but he freely expressed his disappointment with its more regressive aspects, mourning the opportunities that Congress had lost. While Stevens hoped that Congress would see fit to pass more expansive measures—including black suffrage—at a later date, his comments reveal a deep sense of resignation and pessimism.

From Cong. Globe, 39th Cong., 1st Sess., 3148.

We may, perhaps, congratulate the House and the country on the near approach to completion of a proposition to be submitted to the people for the admission of an outlawed community into the privileges and advantages of a civilized and free Government.

When I say that we should rejoice at such completion, I do not thereby intend so much to express joy at the superior excellence of the scheme, as that there is to be a scheme—a scheme containing much positive good, as well, I am bound to admit, as the omission of many better things.

In my youth, in my manhood, in my old age, I had fondly dreamed that when any fortunate chance should have broken up for awhile the foundation of our institutions, and released us from obligations the most tyrannical that ever man imposed in the name of freedom, that the intelligent, pure and just men of this Republic, true to their professions and their consciences, would have so remodeled all our institutions as to have freed them from every vestige of human oppression, of inequality of rights, of the recognized degradation of the poor, and the superior caste of the rich. In short, that no distinction would be tolerated in this purified Republic but what arose from merit and conduct. This bright dream has vanished "like the baseless fabric of a vision." I find that we shall be obliged to be content with patching up the worst portions of the ancient edifice, and leaving it, in many of its parts, to be swept through by the tempests, the frosts, and the storms of despotism.

Do you inquire why, holding these views and possessing some will of my own, I accept so imperfect a proposition? I answer, because I live among men and not among angels; among men as intelligent, as determined, and as independent as myself, who, not agreeing with me, do not choose to yield their opinions to mine. Mutual concession, therefore, is our only resort, or mutual hostilities.

We might well have been justified in making renewed and more strenuous efforts for a better plan could we have had the coöperation of the Executive. With his cordial assistance the rebel States might have been made model republics, and this nation an empire of universal freedom. But he preferred "restoration" to "reconstruction." He chooses that the slave States should remain as nearly as possible in their ancient condition, with such small modifications as he and his prime minister[1] should suggest, without any impertinent interference from Congress. He anticipated the legitimate action of the national Legislature, and by rank usurpation erected governments in the conquered provinces;

---

[1] Stevens is making a snide reference to Secretary of State William H. Seward.

imposed upon them institutions in the most arbitrary and unconstitutional manner; and now maintains them as legitimate governments, and insolently demands that they shall be represented in Congress on equal terms with loyal and regular States. . . .

You perceive that while I see much good in the proposition I do not pretend to be satisfied with it. And yet I am anxious for its speedy adoption, for I dread delay. The danger is that before any constitutional guards shall have been adopted Congress will be flooded by rebels and rebel sympathizers. . . . Hence, I say, let us no longer delay; take what we can get now, and hope for better things in further legislation[.]

25

The Fourteenth Amendment to the U.S. Constitution

1868

The Fourteenth Amendment to the U.S. Constitution — the second of the so-called Reconstruction Amendments — passed Congress on June 13, 1866. The required three-quarters of the states had ratified the amendment by July 1868.

In an echo of the Civil Rights Bill, the amendment's first section defined the basis of citizenship and codified the principle of legal equality before the law. The first section of the Fourteenth Amendment has formed the basis of an extraordinary body of jurisprudence since ratification. The second section decreased congressional representation for states that denied the right to vote to a portion of their population on the basis of race. This section also introduced the word male *to the Constitution, a provision that frustrated women's rights activists. The third section prevented Confederates who had previously served in the U.S. government from holding office. The fourth section prevented payment of Confederate war debt. The fifth section gave Congress the power of enforcement.*

From Edward McPherson, *The Political History of the United States of America during the Period of Reconstruction* (Washington, D.C.: Philp & Solomons, 1871), 102.

SECTION 1. All persons born or naturalized in the United States, and subject to the jurisdiction thereof, are citizens of the United States and of the State wherein they reside. No State shall make or enforce any law which shall abridge the privileges or immunities of citizens of the United States; nor shall any State deprive any person of life, liberty, or property, without due process of law, nor deny to any person within its jurisdiction the equal protection of the laws.

SEC 2. Representatives shall be apportioned among the several States according to their respective numbers, counting the whole number of persons in each State, excluding Indians not taxed. But when the right to vote at any election for the choice of electors for President and Vice-President of the United States, representatives in Congress, the executive and judicial officers of a State, or the members of the legislature thereof, is denied to any of the male inhabitants of such State, being twenty-one years of age, and citizens of the United States, or in any way abridged, except for participation in rebellion or other crime, the basis of representation therein shall be reduced in the proportion which the number of such male citizens shall bear to the whole number of male citizens twenty-one years of age in such State.

SEC 3. No person shall be a senator or representative in Congress, or elector of President and Vice-President, or hold any office, civil or military, under the United States, or under any State, who, having previously taken an oath, as a member of Congress, or as an officer of the United States, or as a member of any State legislature, or as an executive or judicial officer of any State, to support the Constitution of the United States, shall have engaged in insurrection or rebellion against the same, or given aid or comfort to the enemies thereof. But Congress may, by a vote of two-thirds of each house, remove such disability.

SEC 4. The validity of the public debt of the United States, authorized by law, including debts incurred for payment of pensions and bounties for services in suppressing insurrection or rebellion, shall not be questioned. But neither the United States nor any State shall assume or pay any debt or obligation incurred in aid of insurrection or rebellion against the United States, or any claim for the loss or emancipation of any slave; but all such debts, obligations and claims shall be held illegal and void.

SEC 5. The Congress shall have power to enforce, by appropriate legislation, the provisions of this article.

26

WENDELL PHILLIPS

Speech Criticizing the Fourteenth Amendment

October 25, 1866

In his postwar speeches and writings, abolitionist Wendell Phillips consistently advocated a Radical approach to Reconstruction. When Congress approved the Fourteenth Amendment in June 1866, Phillips was appalled. The amendment failed to incorporate black men's suffrage, instead allowing states to accept reduced representation in exchange for the maintenance of an all-white electorate. Phillips also took issue with the amendment's use of the word male, *which marked the first time such gendered language had been employed in the Constitution. He critiqued the amendment and congressional Republicans in a speech at the Cooper Institute in New York City. Phillips's frustration with "compromise" offers an important reminder that Radical Republicans were never able to dictate Reconstruction policy. Their alliance with moderate and conservative Republicans made it possible to pass legislation, but it also limited the lengths to which Radicals could go in their attempt to remake the South.*

This amendment, which we are told by the official voice—and that is the only one to which we can listen—is to be a bridge to restore the South to its old [place] in the Government, undertakes, in the first place, to engraft into the Constitution of the United States a new feature. As the nineteenth century opens before us the largest and most progressive minds of both continents are undertaking to enlarge the political arena, while both sections of the United States stand ready to-day to expand with the opening demands of the nineteenth century. [Yet], the timid and cowardly policy of a party bound only upon its own perpetuation, undertakes to engraft into that Constitution the word "male," confining us in the onward march of the suffrage question to one sex. I repudiate all limitations. [Applause.] Our fathers left it uncommitted to face the demands of the opening century. I would leave it uncommitted. The

From "Mr. Wendell Phillips on the Administration and the Republican Party," *New York Tribune*, 26 October 1866, 8.

amendment, secondly, undertakes to ignore entirely the rights of the negro to the help of the Government. To-day we have the right to protect him, and the power. The amendment surrenders both into the hands of the dominant race of the Southern Territories. We have to-day the right, gained by battle, and we have the power, having the whole Government machinery in our hands. We are pledged in honor, and by the necessities of a five years' war, to exercise both the right and the power. The Republican party undertakes to give up the right and the power. . . . They call it a *compromise*. Compromise is a respectable word. It covers a respectable fact. Compromise is when two men differ on a boundary and agree to settle it by mutual arrangement. Compromise is when two men disagree on the amount due each on a contract or from the profits of a business, and they sit down and arrange their mutual claims, honorable, just and equal. There never has been a compromise in American political history. We have elevated a *swindle* into a compromise and dignified with the name. . . . The House of Representatives and Senate essayed to amend the Constitution in safety, because 4,000,000 of blacks held their places in the scale when the balance trembled beneath the North and South, and they sat down with a Rebel President[1] to swindle their allies out of their rights, and gave the amendment to the country as a compromise. . . . The Constitutional amendment, so far as the negro is concerned, is a swindle, and don't delude anybody with the respectable but misused term of "compromise." The absent, the unheard, the disfranchised race is sacrificed between the upper and nether millstone of Rebeldom, while the Republican party knowingly, systematically and persistently sacrifice it to preserve their political supremacy.

---

[1] Phillips is referring to Andrew Johnson.

27

Resolutions of the North Carolina Freedmen's Convention

October 1866

Even before they gained the right to vote, southern freedpeople embraced the political sphere. Conventions like the one held in Raleigh, North Carolina, in October 1866 were quite common in the Reconstruction South. Over four days of meetings, convention delegates heard speeches on topics including education, labor relations, racial violence, and the Republican party. In a series of resolutions, delegates praised congressional Republicans for their support of black civil rights, while urging them to extend the franchise to African Americans. As they kept one eye on Washington, however, they also looked closer to home, establishing several institutions to organize black self-defense and political activity at the local level.

WHEREAS, In the Counties of Jones, Duplin, Wayne, Craven, Hyde, Halifax, and others in this State, outrages are being committed, such as killing, shooting, and robbing the unprotected people, for the most trivial offence, and, in many instances, for no offence at all; and, whereas, those criminals who [commit] these fiendish outrages are allowed to roam freely at large without being arrested for their crimes; therefore,

1. *Be it resolved*, That the colored people in every county, district and village throughout the State form themselves into auxiliary leagues, which leagues must be connected with the State organization, its bureau to be located in Raleigh, N. C., and whose duty it shall be to receive reports of outrages from auxiliary leagues, or from the people of said counties, &c., and communicate them to headquarters, and such newspapers throughout the count[r]y as it may deem proper, so that the government and the world may know of the cruelties inflicted upon us and the disadvantages under which we labor.

2. *Resolved*, That the representatives of the colored people of North-Carolina fully appreciate, with profound gratitude, and endorse the action of the 39th Congress in the passage of the Freedmen's Bureau

From *Minutes of the Freedmen's Convention held in the City of Raleigh on the 2nd, 3rd, 4th, and 5th of October, 1866* (Raleigh: Standard Book and Job Office, 1866), 14–15.

bill, Civil Rights bill, and the Constitutional amendment. Hoping that a like spirit of justice and humanity may guide the acts of their 40th session, until legislation shall protect equally the rights of all American people, without regard to race or color, for which we shall ever pray.

3. *Whereas,* The unreconstructed States regard taxation without representation unjust, and not in conformity with a Republican form of government; therefore,

Be it resolved, That we native born colored citizens of North-Carolina regard the same principle as applicable to us in every relation. . . .

5. *Resolved,* That it shall be the duty of every member of the Convention on returning home to form or cause to be formed an Equal Rights League in or near the place wherein such member shall reside, and to do all in his power to promote their increase throughout other portions of his county. . . .

9. *Resolved,* That a vote of thanks be tendered to the honorable Chas. Sumner, Thaddeus Stevens, Wade, Trumbull, H. Greel[e]y[1] and to Fred. Douglas[s], Henry H. Garnet and other beacon lights of our race.

---

[1] Horace Greeley was the editor of the *New York Tribune* and an outspoken opponent of slavery.

3

Toward African American Suffrage

28

Record of Ratification Votes for the Fourteenth Amendment

October 1866–February 1867

Although Congress had not clarified the procedure by which the southern states might regain their seats in the House and Senate, it was clear that ratification of the Fourteenth Amendment was a necessary first step. And yet, when the amendment went to the states for ratification in late 1866, Tennessee was the only former Confederate state to give its approval. One by one, southern state legislatures voted the amendment down. In several states the vote was unanimous; in all of them, the majorities against ratification were enormous.

The defeat of the amendment in the former Confederacy empowered Radical forces in Congress. The votes offered undeniable evidence of the South's continuing hostility to federally controlled Reconstruction. Republican moderates began to align themselves with the political program of the Radicals. Southern actions solidified Republican opinion in Congress, opening the door for African American suffrage.

INSURRECTIONARY STATES.
REJECTED—TEN STATES.
Virginia—
    SENATE, January 9, 1867, unanimously.
    HOUSE, January 9, 1867, 1 for amendment.

From Edward McPherson, *The Political History of the United States of America during the Period of Reconstruction* (Washington, D.C.: Philp & Solomons, 1871), 194.

North Carolina—
  SENATE, December 13, 1866, yeas 1, nays 44.
  HOUSE, December 13, 1866, yeas 10, nays 93.

South Carolina—
  SENATE, ——— ———.
  HOUSE, December 20, 1866, yeas 1, nays 95.

Georgia—
  SENATE, November 9, 1866, yeas 0, nays 36.
  HOUSE, November 9, 1866, yeas 2, nays 131.

Florida—
  SENATE, December 3, 1866, yeas 0, nays 20.
  HOUSE, December 1, 1866, yeas 0, nays 49.

Alabama—
  SENATE, December 7, 1866, yeas 2, nays 27.
  HOUSE, December 7, 1866, yeas 8, nays 69.

Mississippi—
  SENATE, January 30, 1867, yeas 0, nays 27.
  HOUSE, January 25, 1867, yeas 0, nays 88.

Louisiana—
  SENATE, February 5, 1867, unanimously.
  HOUSE, February 6, 1867, unanimously.

Texas—
  SENATE, ——— ———.
  HOUSE, October 13, 1866, yeas 5, nays 67.

Arkansas—
  SENATE, December 15, 1866, yeas 1, nays 24.
  HOUSE, December 17, 1866, yeas 2, nays 68.

29

THOMAS NAST

"King Andy"

November 3, 1866

The Thomas Nast cartoon shown here appeared in Harper's Weekly
*shortly before the 1866 midterm elections. In an attempt to secure votes
for the Republicans, Nast depicted the president as a brutal tyrant willing
to destroy American democracy in order to best his political adversaries. Thaddeus Stevens has his head on the chopping block, while Charles
Sumner is the third man standing in line. Partially due to Johnson's
erratic behavior, the Republicans scored important gains in the 1866
congressional elections.*

94

30

ANDREW JOHNSON

Second Annual Message
December 3, 1866

In the fall elections of 1866, congressional Republicans campaigned behind the Fourteenth Amendment. Andrew Johnson did all he could to unseat his Republican adversaries. Faced with a choice between Johnson's "restoration" and the congressional program of Reconstruction, northern voters returned Republican candidates by huge margins. Republicans would enjoy a veto-proof majority when the next Congress assembled in March 1867.

When Johnson prepared his annual message to Congress in December, however, he showed neither humility nor resignation. Johnson criticized Republican members of Congress for their continued unwillingness to seat the "loyal Senators and Representatives" of the South. From Johnson's perspective, the process of Reconstruction was all but complete. The federal government had neither the right nor the obligation to involve itself further in southern affairs. Congress should seat the duly elected claimants from the South so the nation could move on.

Johnson's message was woefully out of touch with the prevailing currents of thought in Congress. Congressional Republicans had no intention of restoring the states of the former Confederacy to full representation until they had proven themselves worthy of it. Armed with a veto-proof majority, congressional Republicans would begin Reconstruction anew, hoping to create a South that was truly loyal, just, and egalitarian.

After a brief interval the Congress of the United States resumes its annual legislative labors. An all-wise and merciful Providence has abated the pestilence which visited our shores, leaving its calamitous traces upon some portions of our country. Peace, order, tranquillity, and civil authority have been formally declared to exist throughout the whole of the United States. In all of the States civil authority has superseded the

---

From Edward McPherson, *The Political History of the United States of America during the Period of Reconstruction* (Washington, D.C.: Philp & Solomons, 1871), 143–45.

coercion of arms, and the people, by their voluntary action, are maintaining their governments in full activity and complete operation. . . . An entire restoration of fraternal feeling must be the earnest wish of every patriotic heart; and we will have accomplished our grandest national achievement when, forgetting the sad events of the past, and remembering only their instructive lessons, we resume our onward career as a free, prosperous, and united people. . . .

I deem it a subject of profound regret that Congress has thus far failed to admit to seats loyal Senators and Representatives from the other States whose inhabitants, with those of Tennessee, had engaged in the rebellion.[1] Ten States—more than one-fourth of the whole number—remain without representation. The seats of fifty members in the House of Representatives and of twenty members in the Senate are yet vacant—not by their own consent, not by a failure of election, but by the refusal of Congress to accept their credentials. . . .

It is true, it has been assumed that the existence of the States was terminated by the rebellious acts of their inhabitants, and that the insurrection having been suppressed, they were thenceforward to be considered merely as conquered territories. The legislative, executive, and judicial departments of the Government have, however, with great distinctness and uniform consistency, refused to sanction an assumption so incompatible with the nature of our republican system and with the professed objects of the war. Throughout the recent legislation of Congress, the undeniable fact makes itself apparent, that these ten political communities are nothing less than States of this Union. . . .

I know of no measure more imperatively demanded by every consideration of national interest, sound policy, and equal justice, than the admission of loyal members from the now unrepresented States. This would consummate the work of restoration, and exert a most salutary influence in the re-establishment of peace, harmony, and fraternal feeling. It would tend greatly to renew the confidence of the American people in the vigor and stability of their institutions. It would bind us more closely together as a nation, and enable us to show to the world the inherent and recuperative power of a Government founded upon the will of the people, and established upon the principles of liberty, justice, and intelligence. Our increased strength and enhanced prosperity would irrefragably[2] demonstrate the fallacy of the arguments

[1] The contingent from Tennessee was seated after the state ratified the Fourteenth Amendment.
[2] Indisputably.

against free institutions drawn from our recent national disorders by the enemies of republican government. The admission of loyal members from the States now excluded from Congress, by allaying doubt and apprehension, would turn capital, now awaiting an opportunity for investment, into the channels of trade and industry. It would alleviate the present troubled condition of those States, and, by inducing emigration, aid in the settlement of fertile regions now uncultivated, and lead to an increased production of those staples which have added so greatly to the wealth of the nation and the commerce of the world. New fields of enterprise would be opened to our progressive people, and soon the devastations of war would be repaired, and all traces of our domestic differences effaced from the minds of our countrymen.

31

FREDERICK DOUGLASS

"Reconstruction"

December 1866

Frederick Douglass was the most well-known black leader of the Civil War era. Born a slave in Maryland, Douglass escaped to the North in 1838. He became an extraordinarily popular abolitionist speaker. In 1845, he published his Narrative of the Life of Frederick Douglass. *During the war, Douglass pressured the Lincoln administration to embrace the cause of freedom and took the lead in encouraging the enlistment of black troops after the Emancipation Proclamation. During Reconstruction, Douglass was a vocal supporter of civil equality and African American suffrage. In this article, published in the aftermath of the Republican victories in the election of 1866, Douglass laid out his vision of Reconstruction and urged Congress to embrace a Radical policy. Equal suffrage, Douglass argued, was the only way to secure the desired transformation in the South. The people of the North had made their position clear; Congress must fulfill its mandate.*

From Frederick Douglass, "Reconstruction," *Atlantic Monthly*, December 1866, 761, 763–65.

The assembling of the Second Session of the Thirty-ninth Congress may very properly be made the occasion of a few earnest words on the already much-worn topic of reconstruction.

Seldom has any legislative body been the subject of a solicitude more intense, or of aspirations more sincere and ardent. There are the best of reasons for this profound interest. Questions of vast moment, left undecided by the last session of Congress, must be manfully grappled with by this. No political skirmishing will avail. The occasion demands statesmanship.

Whether the tremendous war so heroically fought and so victoriously ended shall pass into history a miserable failure, barren of permanent results,—a scandalous and shocking waste of blood and treasure, . . . or whether, on the other hand, we shall, as the rightful reward of victory over treason, have a solid nation, entirely delivered from all contradictions and social antagonisms, based upon loyalty, liberty, and equality, must be determined one way or the other by the present session of Congress. . . .

If time was at first needed, Congress has now had time. All the requisite materials from which to form an intelligent judgment are now before it. Whether its members look at the origin, the progress, the termination of the war, or at the mockery of a peace now existing, they will find only one unbroken chain of argument in favor of a radical policy of reconstruction. . . . The members go to Washington fresh from the inspiring presence of the people. In every considerable public meeting, and in almost every conceivable way, whether at court-house, school-house, or cross-roads, in doors and out, the subject has been discussed, and the people have emphatically pronounced in favor of a radical policy. Listening to the doctrines of expediency and compromise with pity, impatience, and disgust, they have everywhere broken into demonstrations of the wildest enthusiasm when a brave word has been spoken in favor of equal rights and impartial suffrage. Radicalism, so far from being odious, is now the popular passport to power. . . .

It is not, however, within the scope of this paper to point out the precise steps to be taken, and the means to be employed. The people are less concerned about these than the grand end to be attained. They demand such a reconstruction as shall put an end to the present anarchical state of things in the late rebellious States,—where frightful murders and wholesale massacres are perpetrated in the very presence of Federal soldiers. This horrible business they require shall cease. They want a reconstruction such as will protect loyal men, black and white, in their persons and property; such a one as will cause Northern industry,

Northern capital, and Northern civilization to flow into the South, and make a man from New England as much at home in Carolina as elsewhere in the Republic. No Chinese wall can now be tolerated. The South must be opened to the light of law and liberty, and this session of Congress is relied upon to accomplish this important work.

The plain, common-sense way of doing this work, as intimated at the beginning, is simply to establish in the South one law, one government, one administration of justice, one condition to the exercise of the elective franchise, for men of all races and colors alike. This great measure is sought as earnestly by loyal white men as by loyal blacks, and is needed alike by both. Let sound political prescience but take the place of an unreasoning prejudice, and this will be done.

32

HAMILTON WARD

Speech on Radical Republicanism

December 13, 1866

Hamilton Ward was a Radical congressman from New York. In this speech on the floor of Congress, he insisted that the Republican victory in the elections of 1866 should be read as a mandate for a more Radical congressional policy. Ward offered a full-throated defense of Radicalism, urging Congress to embrace African American suffrage and to dissolve the southern state governments established during Presidential Reconstruction. Ward expressed an overriding faith in the power of the ballot, concluding his speech with a utopian vision of a nation reformed and rejuvenated through an embrace of egalitarian democracy. Although Ward was not as well known as fellow representatives Thaddeus Stevens or George Julian, this speech stands as a remarkable example of Radical political thought at a formative moment in the Reconstruction process.

From Hamilton Ward Jr., ed., *The Life and Speeches of Hamilton Ward, 1829–1898* (Buffalo, N.Y.: A. H. Morey, 1902), 105, 107, 109–11, 114, 116–17.

The country has spoken; the popular verdict stands recorded in the recent elections; and the Thirty-Ninth Congress reassembles strengthened, encouraged, and instructed by the great tribunal to which it appealed, the loyal people of the United States. . . .

Then away with your timid conservatism; away with that quality that would compromise the right, that would barter away equality, justice, and plighted faith for expediency, trade, and the good-will of traitors. I am sick of your expediency men and measures; the times demand radical men and measures. Radicalism crowded the Mayflower, landed on Plymouth Rock, dotted settlements along the Atlantic coast, declared "not one cent for tribute, but millions for defense," threw the tea into Boston Harbor, made the immortal Declaration, achieved our independence, redeemed this great land from the wilderness, built the school house and the church, covered the land with cities and towns, and the ocean with ships, stretched the electric cord through the great waters so that continent talked with continent under the sea, sent two million men to the front, crushed out the rebellion, kept traitors out of Congress, repudiated Andrew Johnson, the rebels, and Copperheads by more than half a million majority, and now it proposes to reap all the fruits of the great victories of the sword and the ballot-box by reconstructing the Republic upon a sound and just basis so that it will stand forever. . . .

But we are told that those ten States are reorganized, that they have State governments. I am aware that there are rebel machines in the territory recently in rebellion that call themselves States. I am aware that the President has undertaken to galvanize them into States by proclamation, but no good lawyer will for a moment contend that these organizations have any validity as State governments until they are recognized as valid by Congress. They are monstrous systems of fraud, oppression, and murder. They exclude from power all men loyal to the Union. They screen from merited punishment the assassins of ten thousand loyal men who have been butchered in their territory since they "accepted the situation."[1] They deny to Union men and freedmen that which the Constitution guarantees to them. . . .

Ah, Mr. Chairman, we have neglected the duty too long of formally rejecting these creatures of treason. We must begin the work anew and provide by law that all male persons in those States aside from the excepted classes of the age of twenty-one years, nativ[e]-born or

---

[1] In late 1865, Union general Ulysses S. Grant made a brief tour of the South at the request of Andrew Johnson. Grant reported that "the mass of thinking men of the South accepted the situation in good faith."

naturalized, shall have the right to vote in electing delegates to conventions to frame new State constitutions or amend old ones, in electing State, legislative and judicial officers, and all other elections that may occur in the reorganization of these State governments; that no person who has engaged in rebellion shall be eligible to office in the new State organization or in the conventions aforesaid. . . .

But, Mr. Chairman, it will be said that I am in favor of universal negro suffrage at the South. Indeed, sir, I am. The ballot is the only protection after all that men have in this country. Take the ballot away from a class and that class will not have equal rights with those who do exercise the ballot. Your civil rights bill is well, necessary, but what avail it unless it is enforced. Put it into the Constitution as you will, and as you should, but it will be as a rainbow in the cloud to the oppressed people of the South without there is some power there to enforce it. . . .

Adopt the plan I propose and all the States will be represented in the next Congress, the murder, persecution, and banishment of Union men will cease. The Constitution, the civil rights bill, and all other provisions of law for the protection of the people of the South will be a living fact realized in every portion of the South, for everywhere the loyal man will be clothed with the power of enforcing those rights. . . .

The South will cease to be a section and become a part of the nation; her sons and daughters shall build altars to freedom in her waste places; the wilderness shall vanish, the church and school-house will appear; and light and knowledge will illumine her dark corners; freedom of speech, of opinion, and of the press will be as much secured in South Carolina as in Maine; all men shall be citizens, and high and clear in the fundamental law will that charter of citizenship be found guiding the nation like a pillar of flame; the whole land will revive under the magic touch of free labor, and we shall arise from the ashes of the rebellion to a purer life and a higher destiny, illustrating the grand truth of man's capacity for self-government; then Columbia[2] will march on through the ages that are to come, her navies triumphant on every sea, her commerce encircling the earth, her arms the terror of tyrants and the hope of slaves, her influence ascendant in every capital; the oppressed of all nations will come to our shores, and free governments everywhere be founded from the inspiration of our example; firm upon the rock of justice and equality the temple reared by our fathers and purified by the blood of our brothers shall stand in the midst of the wondering nations, the most potent, free and glorious of all. Shall this be so? It is ours to say.

---

[2] Columbia was a female figure that symbolized the United States.

33

JOHN BROOMALL

Speech on Black Suffrage

January 8, 1867

*As the House of Representatives began debates on the legislation that
would become the Reconstruction Act of 1867, Pennsylvania Radical
John Broomall offered a bold call for black suffrage. For Broomall, the
ballot promised an important means of self-defense for southern African
Americans. In his speech, Broomall made explicit reference to two brutal
massacres that convulsed the South in 1866. In May, a white mob in
Memphis, Tennessee, had burned black homes and killed dozens of African Americans over three days of violence. (See Document 22.) In July, a
Republican political convention in New Orleans had offered a pretext for
white Confederate veterans to attack black and white Republicans in the
street. Such events, Broomall insisted, were far from exceptional.*

*Broomall—like Hamilton Ward—placed great emphasis on the ballot.
The suffrage offered an appealing, if simplistic, answer to an extraordinarily difficult problem. Armed with the vote, Republicans thought,
African Americans could hold elected leaders accountable, thereby protecting themselves from the violent passions of southern white supremacists.
Subsequent events—from the violence of the Ku Klux Klan to the legalized
segregation of the late nineteenth century—would prove this faith misguided. From the perspective of early 1867, however, black suffrage seemed
an ideal solution to the South's racial crisis.*

[G]entlemen on the other side of the House say that this is a white
man's Government, and they raise their hands with an affectation of
holy horror at the idea of extending political rights to the negroes. Do
they not know that our Government is emphatically the Government of
the governed? And are none but white men governed by it? Do they not
know that at the time of the adoption of our Constitution negroes voted
in every State of the Union but one? Do they not know that members of
the Convention that framed that instrument were voted for by negroes,

From Cong. Globe, 39th Cong., 2d Sess., 351.

and that there was no law and no principle of our institutions which would have prevented a negro from sitting in that convention if he had been duly elected? Do they not know that there is not now and that there never has been any law to prevent a negro from holding the office of President of the United States if he should be otherwise qualified? . . .

There is doubtless a great degree of ignorance among the negroes of the South; but who is responsible for it? Not they. Until recently it was a crime punishable by fine and imprisonment in every one of the States lately in rebellion to teach negroes to read. Even the Bible was by law a sealed book to them. Certain portions of it, selected with especial reference to the pecuniary advantage of their masters, might be read to them by judicious ministers of the Gospel; but if some simple-minded philanthropist should attempt to open its full light upon their benighted understandings it would be well for him if he could obtain the advantage of the punishment meted to his crime by law, and thereby avoid the hemp and the bowie-knife.

But I deny that any man should be deprived of political rights on account of his ignorance. Governments are intended to equalize, as far as possible, the weak with the strong, the poor with the rich, the ignorant with the intelligent. Political rights are intended to enable men to preserve that portion of their natural rights which is the especial object of government; that is to say their civil rights of life, liberty, and property; and the only valid reason that can be urged for denying political rights to any man is that he is capable of preserving his civil rights without them.

Can the negro in the South preserve his civil rights without political ones? Let the convention riot of New Orleans answer; let the terrible three days in Memphis answer. In the latter city three hundred negroes who had periled their lives in the service of their country and still wore its uniform, were compelled to look on while the officers of the law, elected by white men, set their dwellings in flames and fired upon their wives and children as they escaped from the doors and windows. Their churches and school-houses were burned because they were their churches and school-houses. Outrages which the tongue refuses to describe in language, were perpetrated upon their women; and the dead mother, who was killed because she resisted, and her living child were thrown together into the flames of the building that was burned because it afforded them a home. Yet no arrest, no conviction, no punishment awaits the perpetrators of these deeds, who walk in open day and boast of their enormities, because, forsooth, this is a white man's Government.

Let it not be said that these occurrences are unusual and extraordinary. The history of the last eighteen months will exhibit their parallel in every State and in every city of the subjugated South; and the present organizations in that territory, the base offspring of northern perfidy and southern treason, cannot, and will not, afford the adequate remedy. It is quite time that this government should recognize the rights of the black man, and should arm him with the ballot, that he may not be compelled to arm himself with the pistol and the knife in defense of those whom his duty to his God requires that he should defend.

34

JAMES M. ASHLEY

Speech on the Southern State Governments
January 26, 1867

In this speech, delivered during the debates preceding the Reconstruction Act, Ohio Radical James M. Ashley called for the nullification of the state governments elected during Presidential Reconstruction. Ashley claimed that Andrew Johnson had overstepped his authority when he allowed the southern states to reconstitute themselves in 1865; this had been Congress's right and responsibility. As such, the governments ruling in the South were "illegal and void." Again and again, these governments had refused to accommodate themselves to emancipation, Reconstruction, and African American civil rights. Ashley demanded that Congress take bold action, doing whatever was necessary to provide the states of the South with governments that truly represented the will of the people. Before a true Reconstruction of the South could occur, Ashley insisted, Johnson's false and corrupt governments had to be stripped of their authority.

From *Duplicate Copy of the Souvenir from the Afro-American League of Tennessee to Hon. James M. Ashley of Ohio* (n.p.: Afro-American League of Tennessee, 1893), 416, 426–27, 434–35.

The Thirty-ninth Congress went to the country in opposition to the policy of the President, and to what we were pleased to denominate his usurpations. The people in generous confidence have sustained Congress and returned to the Fortieth Congress by majorities unprecedented men pledged to the abolition of the governments established by the acting President of the United States, in violation of all law, and, as I claim, in clear violation of the Constitution. A large majority on this side of the House were returned to the next Congress under the express pledge that they would not permit these rebel State governments to exist a single hour after this Congress had been in session long enough to declare them abolished. If this Congress fails to redeem that pledge it will commit a blunder which, in such an hour as this, is worse than a crime. . . .

I suppose there is no one in this House who would claim or admit that the Government of the United States has any constitutional power to authorize or recognize the right of a majority of the people of a State to dissolve their constitutional relations with the General Government. So far as I am concerned, and the great body of the men with whom I act, we utterly deny it. But, sir, if the people of a State do the act, what then? Who is there to prescribe the terms and conditions upon which these States shall be restored when these acts are consummated? . . .

I hold that the people of a State may, and all know that eleven States did, in violation of the Constitution, dissolve their practical relations with the National Government. As an individual citizen may, in violation of law, commit crime, so may a political community, in violation of law, refuse or neglect to discharge their constitutional obligations. If they do this thing, I hold that the States which remain loyal must always represent the national sovereignty and have the right to dictate such terms as they may see fit to revolting States, and to compel the people of the States so violating the Constitution to accept those terms, or to remain during the pleasure of the conqueror in the condition in which we now find the late rebel States. . . .

Sir, all I ask, and all the loyal men of this country ask who have sacrificed so much in blood and treasure in putting down the rebellion, is that in the restoration of these States care shall be taken that the National Government shall not again be imperiled by a counter-revolution, in which the apostate President shall be the leader, aided by the late rebels and their northern allies. Hence I am in favor of prompt and vigorous action by this Congress. I hold that these governments set up by Mr. Johnson are illegal, and I want them declared illegal and void before this Congress adjourns. . . .

I want peace, I want unity, I want the Government restored, but I do not want the men who conquered the rebellion proscribed, and the governments of the rebel States carried on by the men who have been waging bitter war against us for the past four years. I utterly repudiate the assumption of the President that he can parole armies and then authorize these paroled prisoners of war to form constitutional State governments for the loyal men in the States recently in rebellion. . . . I say we are ready to forgive the great body of the Southern people, we are anxious to forgive them; but we are determined, by the grace of God, that these rebel State governments organized by Johnson shall not be recognized, come what may; that disloyal Representatives shall not appear upon this floor, nor shall the electoral votes of such States be counted in any presidential election until constitutional governments have been organized and recognized by the Congress of the United States.

35

GEORGE W. JULIAN

"Regeneration before Reconstruction"
January 28, 1867

In this speech, George W. Julian laid out the case for an extended period of military oversight in the South. Reconstruction was in its second year, but Julian argued that little had changed in the South. Racial violence, political intimidation, and the violation of civil rights were commonplace. Julian had not yet given up hope for a true Reconstruction of the South, but he recognized that the process would take time. Rather than racing to re-seat southern representatives and senators, Congress should "make haste slowly." Julian insisted that the southern states should be governed from Washington for an indeterminate period of time, effectively reducing the states of the former Confederacy to the status of territories. Although Julian's viewpoint was too extreme for all but the most Radical

From *Speeches on Political Questions by George W. Julian* (New York: Hurd and Houghton, 1872), 348–49, 352–54.

congressmen, the Reconstruction Act that Congress passed a little over
a month later reflected many of the larger arguments he made in this
speech.

I believe the time has come for action, and that having this great subject
now before us we should proceed earnestly, and with as little delay as
may be, to mature some measure which may meet the demand of the
people. Nearly two years have elapsed since the close of the war, during
the whole of which time the regions blasted by treason have been subject to the authority of Congress; and yet these regions are still unpro-
vided with any valid civil governments, and no loyal man within their
limits, black or white, is safe in his person or estate. The Civil Rights Act
and the Freedmen's Bureau Bill are set at open defiance, while freedom
of speech and of the press are unknown. The loyal people of these districts, with sorely-tried patience and hopes long deferred, plead with us
for our speedy interposition in their behalf; and even the conquered rebels themselves, who are supreme in this general reign of terror, seem
to be growing weary of their term of lawlessness and misrule. Sir, let us
tolerate no further procrastination; and while we justly hold the President responsible for the trouble and maladministration which now curse
the South and disturb the peace of the country, let us remember that
the national odium already perpetually linked with the name of Andrew
Johnson will be shared by us, if we fail in the great duty which is now
brought to our doors. . . .

[The southern states] are not ready for reconstruction as independent States, on any terms or conditions which Congress might impose;
and I believe the time has come for us to say so. We owe this much
to their misguided people, whose false and feverish hopes have been
kept alive by the course of the Executive and the hesitating policy of
Congress. I think I am safe in saying that if these districts were to-day
admitted as States, with the precise political and social elements which
we know to exist in them, even with their rebel population disfranchised
and the ballot placed in the hands of radical Union men only, irrespective of color, the experiment would be ruinous to the best interests
of their loyal people and calamitous to the nation. The withdrawal of
federal intervention and the unchecked operation of local supremacy
would as fatally hedge up the way of justice and equality as the rebel
ascendancy which now prevails. Why? Simply because no theory of government, no forms of administration, can be trusted, unless adequately

supported by public opinion. The power of the great landed aristocracy in these regions, if unrestrained by power from without, would inevitably assert itself. Its political chemistry, obeying its own laws, would very soon crystallize itself into the same forms of treason and lawlessness which to-day hold their undisturbed empire over the existing loyal element. What these regions need, above all things, is not an easy and quick return to their forfeited rights in the Union, but *government*, the strong arm of power, outstretched from the central authority here in Washington, making it safe for the freedmen of the South, safe for her loyal white men, safe for emigrants from the Old World and from the Northern States to go and dwell there; safe for Northern capital and labor, Northern energy and enterprise, and Northern ideas to set up their habitation in peace, and thus found a Christian civilization and a living democracy amid the ruins of the past. That, sir, is what the country demands and the rebel power needs. To talk about suddenly building up independent States where the material for such structure is fatally wanting, is nonsense. States must *grow*, and to that end their growth must be fostered and protected. The political and social regeneration of the country made desolate by treason is the prime necessity of the hour, and is preliminary to any reconstruction of States. Years of careful pupilage under the authority of the nation may be found necessary, and Congress alone must decide when and upon what conditions the tie rudely broken by treason shall be restored. . . .

The grand interests involved plead with us to "make haste slowly," while voices from the graves of our slaughtered countrymen beseech us to "keep none but loyal men on guard." When the rebels, conscious of the ruin they have wrought, shall wash away their guilt in their tears of genuine contrition, then, and not till then, let us restore them to our embrace.

36

The Reconstruction Act
March 1867

*The Reconstruction Act of 1867, passed in March over Johnson's veto,
fulfilled a number of Republican goals. The act divided the former Confederacy (excluding Tennessee) into five military districts. The act did not
dissolve the existing state governments of the South, but it did make them
"provisional" and subject to military authority. At the same time, the act
established a clear process by which the southern states could regain their
seats in Congress. The act required the states to rewrite their constitutions
and to ratify the Fourteenth Amendment. These steps taken, they would
once again be eligible for full political participation on the national level.
The Reconstruction Act marked the height of congressional Radicalism,
but it also foretold the end of federal oversight of the South.*

*The Reconstruction Act instituted African American suffrage in the
South. Its fifth section declared that delegates to the state constitutional
conventions must be elected on the basis of universal manhood suffrage.
In addition, the constitutions these conventions produced were required
to recognize the right to vote regardless of race. The enfranchisement
of southern freedmen completed the social and political revolution that
emancipation had inaugurated, giving birth to a color-blind democracy
in a region barely four years removed from slavery.*

AN ACT to provide for the more efficient government of the rebel States.

Whereas no legal State governments or adequate protection for life
or property now exists in the rebel States of Virginia, North Carolina,
South Carolina, Georgia, Mississippi, Alabama, Louisiana, Florida,
Texas, and Arkansas; and whereas it is necessary that peace and good
order should be enforced in said States until loyal and republican State
governments can be legally established: Therefore,

Be it enacted &c., That said rebel States shall be divided into military
districts and made subject to the military authority of the United States
as hereinafter prescribed, and for that purpose Virginia shall constitute

From Edward McPherson, *The Political History of the United States of America during the
Period of Reconstruction* (Washington, D.C.: Philp & Solomons, 1871), 191–92.

the first district; North Carolina and South Carolina the second district; Georgia, Alabama, and Florida the third district; Mississippi and Arkansas the fourth district; and Louisiana and Texas the fifth district.

SEC. 2. That it shall be the duty of the President to assign to the command of each of said districts an officer of the army, not below the rank of brigadier general, and to detail a sufficient military force to enable such officer to perform his duties and enforce his authority within the district to which he is assigned.

SEC. 3. That it shall be the duty of each officer assigned as aforesaid to protect all persons in their rights of person and property, to suppress insurrection, disorder, and violence, and to punish, or cause to be punished, all disturbers of the public peace and criminals; and to this end he may allow local civil tribunals to take jurisdiction of and to try offenders, or, when in his judgment it may be necessary for the trial of offenders, he shall have power to organize military commissions or tribunals for that purpose; and all interference under color of State authority with the exercise of military authority under this act shall be null and void. . . .

SEC. 5. That when the people of any one of said rebel States shall have formed a constitution of government in conformity with the Constitution of the United States in all respects, framed by a convention of delegates elected by the male citizens of said State, twenty one years old and upward, of whatever race, color, or previous condition, who have been resident in said State for one year previous to the day of such election, except such as may be disfranchised for participation in the rebellion, or for felony at common law, and when such constitution shall provide that the elective franchise shall be enjoyed by all such persons as have the qualifications herein stated for electors of delegates, and when such constitution shall be ratified by a majority of the persons voting on the question of ratification who are qualified as electors for delegates, and when such constitution shall have been submitted to Congress for examination and approval, and Congress shall have approved the same, and when said State, by a vote of its legislature elected under said constitution, shall have adopted the amendment to the Constitution of the United States, proposed by the Thirty-ninth Congress, and known as article fourteen, and when said article shall have become a part of the Constitution of the United States, said State shall be declared entitled to representation in Congress, and Senators and Representatives shall be admitted therefrom on their taking the oath prescribed by law, and then and thereafter the preceding sections of this act shall be inoperative in said State: *Provided*, That no person excluded from the privilege of holding office by said proposed amendment to the Constitution of the

United States, shall be eligible to election as a member of the convention to frame a constitution for any of said rebel States, nor shall any such person vote for members of such convention.

SEC. 6. That until the people of said rebel States shall be by law admitted to representation in the Congress of the United States, any civil governments which may exist therein shall be deemed provisional only, and in all respects subject to the paramount authority of the United States at any time to abolish, modify, control, or supersede the same; and in all elections to any office under such provisional governments all persons shall be entitled to vote, and none others, who are entitled to vote under the provisions of the fifth section of this act; and no person shall be eligible to any office under any such provisional governments who would be disqualified from holding office under the provisions of the third article of said constitutional amendment.

37

A. R. WAUD

"The First Vote"

November 16, 1867

Alfred R. Waud, a British-born illustrator, captured the immediate effects of the Reconstruction Act in this Harper's Weekly *sketch, which appeared in late 1867. The image depicts three southern African Americans—a farmer, a businessman, and a soldier—preparing to cast their first ballots. A white man looks on, trying to come to terms with the political revolution under way. Waud's image offers a powerful representation of black suffrage, the single most radical aspect of Radical Reconstruction.*

HARPER'S WEEKLY.

A JOURNAL OF CIVILIZATION.

VOL. XI.—No. 568.]   NEW YORK, SATURDAY, NOVEMBER 16, 1867.   [SINGLE COPIES TEN CENTS.
$4.00 PER YEAR IN ADVANCE.

Entered according to Act of Congress, in the Year 1867, by Harper & Brothers, in the Clerk's Office of the District Court for the Southern District of New York.

"THE FIRST VOTE."—Drawn by A. R. Waud.—[See next Page.]

4

Impeachment and the Election of Grant

38

CHARLES SUMNER AND JOHN SHERMAN

Debate on Land Redistribution

March 11, 1867

*For true Radicals like Charles Sumner, the Reconstruction Act did not
mark an end to Reconstruction, but a new beginning. Sumner quickly
raised the familiar question of land redistribution. He argued that the
Reconstruction Act had laid the groundwork for the South's political
reintegration without attempting to modify the region's social and economic structures. Without land, Sumner argued, African American
political and civil rights would be easily violated. Relying on the "grasp
of war" doctrine, Sumner claimed that Congress had the right—and
the duty—to complete the work it had started.*

*More moderate Republicans, however, disagreed. Ohio senator John
Sherman was an influential moderate. While Sherman had supported
the Reconstruction Act, he had no intention of following the Radicals
any further. Armed with the vote, Sherman felt, southern African Americans would be able to fend for themselves. In his response to Sumner,
Sherman claimed that Congress must stand by the policy it had established. Further meddling in southern affairs would be unjust and unwise.
The Senate voted to table Sumner's land resolution. The Reconstruction
Act was the furthest that Republican moderates like Sherman were willing to go.*

From Cong. Globe, 40th Cong., 1st Sess., 50, 54–55.

Mr. SUMNER. . . . Congress has undertaken to provide for the military government of the rebel States, and it has made certain requirements with regard to reconstruction, and there it stops. It has presented no complete system, and it has provided no machinery for reconstruction. The consequence is that all our friends at the South at this moment are in the greatest possible anxiety. . . .

I believe that all who are now familiar with the processes of reconstruction have felt that our work would be incomplete unless in some way or other we secured to the freedmen a piece of land. It is only within a few days that gentlemen fresh from traveling through these States have assured me that nothing pressed upon their minds more, as they saw the condition of things there, than the necessity of such a provision. I believe that the more you reflect upon it, and the more you listen to evidence on the subject, the stronger will be your conclusion on that head.

Do you ask me as to the power of Congress? Again I say you find it precisely where you found the power to confer universal suffrage. To give a homestead to all these freedmen will be no more than to give them the vote. You have done the one, and now you must do the other. We are told that to him that hath shall be given, and as you have already given the ballot, that is in possession, you must go further and give, not only education, but the homestead. Nor must you hesitate for want of power. The time for hesitation has passed. . . .

Mr. SHERMAN. . . . We propose to start again civil governments founded upon universal suffrage in those States, and we have declared that that government shall be founded upon the consent of all the people of those States without regard to race, previous condition, or color.

But now, sir, after we have made that offer, after we have made that stipulation, the Senator, before these people have had an opportunity to act upon it, proposes to revoke that offer and make another one still more onerous in its conditions. He says that it is not onerous or burdensome to take from them their land and distribute it among the former slaves. Why, sir, does such a law exist in Massachusetts? . . . Are there not poor people in Massachusetts as well as rich? Does the Senator propose to seize the property of the rich and scatter it among the poor in order to secure a republican government for the State of Massachusetts? . . .

[The southern people] are now ready and willing to come on such terms and conditions as we have offered them. Shall we now add new conditions and new stipulations not contained in any constitution of any of the States? Shall we destroy and derange property in every southern State, and impose conditions that have not been required of any other State in the United States? That is the only question.

I say, therefore, that under the circumstances by which we are sur-
rounded, this proposition of the Senator from Massachusetts and this
whole debate is injurious to the public interests, because it retards the
great process of reconstruction, which is going on very well.

39

JAMES M. ASHLEY

Speech on Impeachment
March 7, 1867

*By 1867, many Republican congressmen had begun to consider seriously
the impeachment of Andrew Johnson. The president continued to use all
the means at his disposal to block the implementation of congressional
policy on the ground in the South. Some Republicans even feared that
Johnson would attempt to circumvent the legislative branch entirely, effectively staging a coup d'état from the White House.*

*Ohio representative James M. Ashley was an early and outspoken ad-
vocate of impeachment. In early 1867, Ashley introduced impeachment
resolutions in the House of Representatives. In this speech, he laid out the
case for impeachment. Ashley accused Johnson of neglecting the duties of
his office and systematically ignoring the dictates of Congress. According
to Ashley, Johnson's actions had endangered the lives of southern loyalists
and helped to keep the spirit of rebellion alive in the former Confederacy.
Ashley's resolutions were referred to the House Judiciary Committee,
which began the long process of gathering evidence in anticipation of
charges of impeachment.*

[T]he people of this country will never permit any man—certainly
no man who came into the Presidency through the door of assassination—to use the vast powers with which the Executive of this country is clothed in defiance of Congress and the people. That the acting
President has done all this and more will not be seriously denied. His

From *Duplicate Copy of the Souvenir from the Afro-American League of Tennessee to Hon.
James M. Ashley of Ohio* (n.p.: Afro-American League of Tennessee, 1893), 440–44.

usurpations of power have been in clear violation of the Constitution, and many of his acts tend directly to revolution. . . . If any loyal man had doubted before, he could doubt no longer, that while this man remains in the presidential office there can be no tranquility in this country, no security for property, liberty, or life to loyal citizens in the South, no such restoration of this Government as the Union army and the Union citizens of this nation have decreed, no safety for a single hour from rebellion or revolution. . . .

The nation cries out in its agony and calls upon the Congress of the United States to deliver them from the shame and disgrace which the acting President has brought upon them. They demand that the loathing incubus which has blotted our country's history with its foulest blot shall be removed. In the name of loyalty betrayed, of law violated, of the Constitution trampled upon, the nation demands the impeachment and removal of Andrew Johnson. . . .

Before he had been one month in the Presidency he entered into a combination with the enemies of the nation to usurp in their interest the prerogatives of Congress, and sought to bind hand and foot the loyal men of the South, who had aided us in putting down the rebellion, by putting the governments of the South in the hands of their mortal enemies and ours. This with me is enough. When you add to this his other acts, which have become public history, the case for me is complete.

The duty of the President is to execute, not to make laws. His oath requires him to see that the laws are faithfully executed. That the President has neglected or refused to execute many of the laws of Congress no man questions. That he has failed to execute the civil rights bill, nay, that he has not even attempted to execute it, the whole country knows. On the other hand, he has not only failed to execute it, but in most indecent and offensive language he has assailed and denounced the law as unconstitutional.

Sir, in his failure to execute this just and most necessary law the crime of the President becomes perfectly colossal. Since the surrender of Lee and Johnston[1] more than five thousand American citizens, guilty of no crime but love of country, have been murdered by men who were lately in arms against this country.[2] Thousands more have been driven from their homes into exile, while no effort has been made on the part of the executive department of the Government to give them the protection

---

[1] Ashley refers to Confederate generals Robert E. Lee and Joseph E. Johnston. Both surrendered in April 1865.

[2] Ashley does not offer a source for this statistic.

which the law demands and which justice and humanity demand. . . . Sir, there never was a nation on this earth guilty of the infamy of treating its loyal citizens as the President of the United States has treated the loyal men of the South. . . .

Mr. Speaker, I do not hesitate to say that, in view of all the facts before us, if this investigation is not proceeded with, and this man is not put on trial, the provision of the Constitution providing for the impeachment of the President is valueless. Sir, if this man is not impeached, if he is not tried and deposed from the high place which he has disgraced, then no man who may succeed him need ever fear trial and conviction, no matter what his crime.

40

GEORGE S. BOUTWELL

Speech on Impeachment

December 5 and 6, 1867

In late November 1867, the House Judiciary Committee presented its report on impeachment. The committee's majority recommended that the House undertake impeachment proceedings against Andrew Johnson. In this speech, George S. Boutwell, a Radical Republican representative from Massachusetts, explained the majority's position. Beginning with a lengthy overview of the legal case for impeachment, Boutwell eventually turned to the specific charges against Johnson. Boutwell admitted that it would be extraordinarily difficult to impeach Johnson on the basis of any of his individual acts. When they were considered collectively, however, Boutwell believed that the president's misdeeds added up to the "high crimes and misdemeanors" required to impeach. Andrew Johnson had made it his mission to thwart the congressional Reconstruction effort, and he had pursued this end with a single-minded determination for nearly two years. This alone, Boutwell argued, constituted sufficient grounds for impeachment.

From Cong. Globe, 40th Cong., 2d Sess., Appendix, 60–61.

*When the impeachment resolutions were brought to a vote before
the full House of Representatives, however, the measures were soundly
defeated. Although Republicans recognized that Johnson posed a serious threat to the success of their southern policy, most were unwilling to
take the unprecedented step of attempting to remove the sitting president
of the United States. The Radical Republicans' first serious attempt at
impeachment failed spectacularly. When they tried again several months
later, they adopted a narrower, more legalistic set of charges centered on
Johnson's alleged violation of the Tenure of Office Act.*

[T]he offense with which the President is charged, and of which I
believe by history he will ultimately be convicted, is that he used as he
had the opportunity, and misused as necessity and circumstances dic-
tated, the great powers of the nation with which he was intrusted [*sic*],
for the purpose of reconstructing this Government in the interest of the
rebellion, so that henceforth this Union, in its legitimate connection, in
its relations, in its powers, in its historical character, should be merely
the continuation of the Government which was organized at Montgom-
ery and transferred to Richmond.[1]

If, sir, this statement unfolds the nature of the case, there would not
be found a particular specific act which would disclose the whole of the
transaction. It was only by a series of acts, by a succession of events, by
participation direct or indirect in numerous transactions, some of them
open and some of them secret, that this great scheme was carried on
and far on towards its final consummation. . . .

I come now to a brief statement of those acts of the President which
disclose his motives and establish his guilt. First he and his friends
sedulously promulgated the idea that what he did in the year 1865 was
temporary. . . .

Then came his vetoes of the various reconstruction measures. I know
very well that it will be said that the President has the veto power in his
hands. To be sure he has; but it is a power to be exercised, like the discretion of a court, in good faith, for proper purposes, in honest judgment
and good conscience, and not persistently in the execution of a scheme
which is in contravention of the just authority of the legislative branch
of the Government. It was exercised, however, by the President for the

---

[1] Boutwell refers here to the two capitals of the Confederacy.

purpose of preventing reconstruction by congressional agency and by authority of law.

Then came his interference by his message of the 22d of June, 1866,[2] and by other acts, all disclosing and furthering a purpose to prevent the ratification of the pending constitutional amendment, a matter with which, as the Executive of the country, he had no concern whatever. The Constitution provides that the House and the Senate, by specified means, may propose amendments to the Constitution; and if any subject is wholly separated from executive authority or control it is this power to amend the Constitution of the United States. The Constitution reserves this power to Congress and to the people, excluding the President. . . .

Then there is connected with these proceedings other public acts, such as the appointment of provisional governors for North Carolina and the other nine States without any authority of law. . . .

When you bring all these acts together; when you consider what he has said; when you consider what he has done; . . . when you consider that in every public act, as far as we can learn, from May, 1865, to the present time, all has tended to this great result, the restoration of the rebels to power under and in the Government of the country; when you consider all these things, can there be any doubt as to his purpose, or doubt as to the criminality of his purpose and his responsibility under the Constitution?

It may not be possible, by specific charge, to arraign him for this great crime, but is he therefore to escape? These offenses which I have enumerated, which are impeachable—and I have enumerated but a part of them—are the acts, the individual acts, the subordinate crimes, the tributary offenses to the accomplishment of the great object which he had in view. But if, upon the body of the testimony, you are satisfied of his purpose, and if you are satisfied that these tributary offenses were committed as the means of enabling him to accomplish this great crime, will you hesitate to try him and convict him upon those charges of which he is manifestly guilty, even if they appear to be of inferior importance, knowing that they were in themselves misdemeanors, that they were tributary offenses, and that in this way, and in this way only, can you protect the State against the final consummation of his crime? We have not yet seen the end of this contest.

---

[2] On this date, Johnson sent a special message to Congress criticizing the Fourteenth Amendment.

41

The Tenure of Office Act
March 2, 1867

*With the apparent failure of the impeachment movement, Andrew John-
son resumed his campaign of disruption. As commander in chief of the
military, Johnson had the power to appoint the officials who would take
charge of the South under the Reconstruction Act. Johnson removed com-
manders known for their sympathy toward African Americans and the
Radical program, replacing them with conservatives disinclined to use
their powers to protect the civil and political rights of black and white
loyalists.*

*In order to complete his triumph, consigning the congressional Re-
construction plan to death by nonaction, Johnson would need to remove
Edwin Stanton, the Radical-leaning secretary of war. However, as a
cabinet-level appointee, Stanton enjoyed the protection of the Tenure of
Office Act. The act, passed in March 1867, required the president to seek
consent of the Senate before removing certain high-ranking officials. In
the summer of 1867, with Congress out of session, Johnson suspended
Stanton. In December, he sent the Senate a justification of his actions,
in conformity with the requirements of the Tenure of Office Act. In early
1868, the Senate rejected the dismissal of Stanton and demanded that
he be reinstated as the secretary of war. On February 21, 1868, Johnson
removed Stanton again, in open defiance of the Tenure of Office Act. In
so doing, Johnson gave advocates of impeachment the very thing they
needed—a clear violation of a specific law, which provided them with
the legal grounds for impeachment.*

AN ACT regulating the tenure of certain civil offices.

*Be it enacted by the Senate and House of Representatives of the United
States of America in Congress assembled,* That every person holding any
civil office to which he has been appointed by and with the advice and
consent of the Senate and every person who shall hereafter be appointed
to any such office, and shall become duly qualified to act therein, is, and

From Edward McPherson, *The Political History of the United States of America during the
Period of Reconstruction* (Washington, D.C.: Philp & Solomons, 1871), 176.

shall be, entitled to hold such office until a successor shall have been in like manner appointed and duly qualified, except as herein otherwise provided: *Provided,* That the Secretaries of State, of the Treasury, of War, of the Navy, and of the Interior, the Postmaster General, and the Attorney General shall hold their offices respectively for and during the term of the President by whom they may have been appointed, and for one month thereafter, subject to removal by and with the advice and consent of the Senate.

42

Articles of Impeachment against Andrew Johnson
March 2, 1868

On February 24, 1868, the House of Representatives voted to impeach Andrew Johnson. Support in the House was not confined to Radical Republicans—moderate and conservative Republicans, reluctant to impeach Johnson in December 1867, now joined with Radicals in supporting the measure. In the following days, the House impeachment managers prepared eleven articles of impeachment. In accordance with the impeachment procedures laid out in the U.S. Constitution, the House managers would present their case to the Senate, which would decide Johnson's guilt or innocence.

In the first three articles, the House impeachment managers laid out the crux of their case against Johnson: the president had violated the Tenure of Office Act in dismissing Stanton; he had also violated the Constitution when he named General Lorenzo Thomas interim secretary of war without the consent of the Senate. Articles IV through IX largely reiterated these charges, while article X accused Johnson of seeking to "bring into disgrace, ridicule, hatred, contempt, and reproach the Congress of the United States" through his speech and action. The eleventh article of impeachment summed up the charges made in earlier articles. Portions of articles I, II, III, and XI are reprinted here.

From Edward McPherson, *The Political History of the United States of America during the Period of Reconstruction* (Washington, D.C.: Philp & Solomons, 1871), 266–67, 270.

Articles exhibited by the House of Representatives of the United States, in the name of themselves and all the people of the United States, against Andrew Johnson, President of the United States, in maintenance and support of their impeachment against him for high crimes and misdemeanors in office.

ARTICLE I.—That the said Andrew Johnson, President of the United States, on the 21st day of February, in the year of our Lord 1868, at Washington, in the District of Columbia, unmindful of the high duties of his office, of his oath of office, and of the requirements of the Constitution that he should take care that the laws be faithfully executed, did unlawfully, and in violation of the Constitution and laws of the United States, issue an order in writing for the removal of Edwin M. Stanton from the office of Secretary for the Department of War, said Edwin M. Stanton having been theretofore duly appointed and commissioned, by and with the advice and consent of the Senate of the United States, as such Secretary. . . . Which order was unlawfully issued with intent then and there to violate the act entitled "An act regulating the tenure of certain civil offices," passed March 2, 1867, . . . whereby said Andrew Johnson, President of the United States, did then and there commit, and was guilty of a high misdemeanor in office.

ARTICLE II.—That on the said 21st day of February, in the year of our Lord one thousand eight hundred and sixty-eight, at Washington, in the District of Columbia, said Andrew Johnson, President of the United States, unmindful of the high duties of his office, of his oath of office, and in violation of the Constitution of the United States, and contrary to the provisions of an act entitled "An act regulating the tenure of certain civil offices," passed March 2, eighteen hundred and sixty-seven, without the advice and consent of the Senate of the United States, said Senate then and there being in session, and without authority of law, did, with intent to violate the Constitution of the United States, and the act aforesaid, issue and deliver to one Lorenzo Thomas a letter of authority, in substance as follows, that is to say:

EXECUTIVE MANSION,
WASHINGTON, D.C., *February* 21, 1868

SIR: The Hon. Edwin M. Stanton having been this day removed from office as Secretary for the Department of War, you are hereby authorized and empowered to act as Secretary of War *ad interim*, and will immediately enter upon the discharge of the duties pertaining to that office.

Mr. Stanton has been instructed to transfer to you all the records, books, papers, and other public property now in his custody and charge.

Respectfully yours,
ANDREW JOHNSON.

To Brevet Major General LORENZO THOMAS,
Adjutant General U.S. Army, Washington, D.C.

Then and there being no vacancy in said office of Secretary for the Department of War, whereby said Andrew Johnson, President of the United States, did then and there commit, and was guilty of a high misdemeanor in office.

ARTICLE III.—That said Andrew Johnson, President of the United States, on the 21st day of February, in the year of our Lord 1868, at Washington, in the District of Columbia, did commit, and was guilty of a high misdemeanor in office, in this, that, without authority of law, while the Senate of the United States was then and there in session, he did appoint one Lorenzo Thomas to be Secretary for the Department of War *ad interim*, without the advice and consent of the Senate, and with intent to violate the Constitution of the United States, no vacancy having happened in said office of Secretary for the Department of War during the recess of the Senate, and no vacancy existing in said office at the time. . . .

ARTICLE XI.—That said Andrew Johnson, President of the United States, unmindful of the high duties of his office, and of his oath of office, and in disregard of the Constitution and laws of the United States, did . . . by public speech, declare and affirm, in substance, that the Thirty-Ninth Congress of the United States was not a Congress of the United States authorized by the Constitution to exercise legislative power under the same, but, on the contrary, was a Congress of only part of the States, thereby denying, and intending to deny, that the legislation of said Congress was valid or obligatory upon him, the said Andrew Johnson, except in so far as he saw fit to approve the same, and also thereby denying, and intending to deny, the power of the said Thirty Ninth Congress to propose amendments to the Constitution of the United States.

43

The Senate Votes on Impeachment
May 1868

The trial of Andrew Johnson lasted more than two months. As its conclusion neared, it became clear that the chances of conviction were slim. Senate Democrats would vote unanimously against conviction, while a number of conservative and moderate Republicans seemed ready to join them. Much of the controversy centered on the fact that Edwin Stanton, an appointee of Abraham Lincoln, may not have been covered under the Tenure of Office Act. If the law did not apply to Stanton, Johnson had not broken it when he dismissed the secretary of war. The House impeachment managers decided to abandon all the articles of impeachment that rested on the Tenure of Office Act. This left the second and third articles—which alleged that Johnson had violated the U.S. Constitution when he named General Lorenzo Thomas interim secretary of war without the consent of the Senate—and the catch-all eleventh article.

On May 16, 1868, the Senate voted on the eleventh article, coming one "guilty" vote short of the two-thirds needed to convict Johnson. Ten days later, the Senate failed to convict Johnson on the second and third articles. In each case, seven Republican senators voted with the Democrats to prevent conviction. Although the failure to convict reflected the weakness of the House's case, more overtly political concerns also played a role. Had Johnson been removed from office, his replacement would have been Benjamin Wade, the president pro tempore of the Senate and a committed Radical. In voting to sustain Johnson, the Republicans who voted "not guilty" were also voting against the expansion of Radical Reconstruction in the South.

May 16—By a vote of 34 to 19, it was ordered that the question on the eleventh article be taken first. . . .

The vote was 35 "guilty," 19 "not guilty," as follow:

GUILTY—Messrs. Anthony, Cameron, Cattell, Chandler, Cole, Conkling, Conness, Corbett, Cragin, Drake, Edmunds, Ferry, Frelinghuysen,

From Edward McPherson, *The Political History of the United States of America during the Period of Reconstruction* (Washington, D.C.: Philp & Solomons, 1871), 282.

Harlan, Howard, Howe, Morgan, Morrill of Maine, Morrill of Vermont, Morton, Nye, Patterson of New Hampshire, Pomeroy, Ramsey, Sherman, Sprague, Stewart, Sumner, Thayer, Tipton, Wade, Willey, Williams, Wilson, Yates—35.

NOT GUILTY—Messrs. *Bayard,*[1] *Buckalew, Davis, Dixon, Doolittle,* Fessenden, Fowler, Grimes, Henderson, *Hendricks, Johnson, McCreery, Norton, Patterson* of Tennessee, Ross, *Saulsbury,* Trumbull, Van Winkle, *Vickers*—19.

May 26—The second and third articles were voted upon, *with the same result as on the eleventh*: GUILTY 35; NOT GUILTY, 19.

A motion that the court do now adjourn *sine die*[2] was then carried—yeas 34, nays 16. . . .

Judgment of acquittal was then entered by the Chief Justice on the three articles voted upon, and the Senate sitting as a court for the trial of Andrew Johnson, President of the United States, upon Articles of Impeachment exhibited by the House of Representatives, was declared adjourned.

44

W. L. SHEPPARD

"Electioneering at the South"

July 25, 1868

With the failure of impeachment, national attention turned to the presidential election of 1868. This image, published in Harper's Weekly *in July 1868, suggests the zeal with which southern African American communities embraced the vote. The drawing depicts a group of African American voters listening to a political speech. In terms of age and economic class, the gathering appears quite diverse. Of particular*

---

[1] Members of the Democratic party are listed in italics.
[2] *Sine die* is Latin for "without day," meaning that the court adjourned without setting a date to reconvene.

significance is the inclusion of several black women. Although both the Reconstruction Act and the Fifteenth Amendment stopped short of female suffrage, African American women embraced the political sphere with a zeal equal to their male counterparts. Such scenes of local black political activism were quite common after 1868, though they would have been unthinkable less than a decade earlier. This is, perhaps, the most noteworthy legacy of Radical Reconstruction.

ELECTIONEERING AT THE SOUTH.—Sketched by W. L. Sheppard.—[See Page 467.]

45

ULYSSES S. GRANT

Acceptance of the 1868 Republican Presidential Nomination

May 1868

In the aftermath of the Johnson impeachment, Republican hopes turned to Ulysses S. Grant, who easily earned the party's 1868 presidential nomination. As the hero of the Union war effort, Grant presented Republicans with a popular candidate who seemed capable of uniting a fractured party. During the election, Grant's political ideology remained something of a mystery. For their part, Radical Republicans feared that his nomination signaled the ascendancy of a more conservative southern policy. Once elected, Grant established himself as a moderate Republican who sought to defend—but not expand upon—the congressional Reconstruction policy he inherited. In the face of increasingly violent white southern resistance to Reconstruction, however, the "peace" for which Grant called in his memorable closing line remained out of reach.

In formally accepting the nomination of the National Republican Convention, it seems that some statement of views beyond the mere acceptance of the nomination should be expressed.

The proceedings of the Convention were marked with wisdom, moderation and patriotism, and I believe express the feelings of the great mass of those who sustained the country through its recent trials. I endorse their resolutions. If elected to the office of President of the United States, it will be my endeavor to administer all the laws in good faith, with economy, and with the view of giving peace, quiet and protection everywhere. In times like the present, it is impossible, or, at least, eminently improper, to lay down a policy to be adhered to, right or wrong, through an administration of four years. New political issues, not foreseen, are constantly arising; the views of the public on old ones are constantly changing, and a purely administrative officer should always

From *Speeches of General U. S. Grant, Republican Candidate for Eighteenth President of the United States, Being Extracts from Speeches, Letters, Orders, Military and State Papers* (Washington, D.C.: Gibson Brothers, 1868), 16.

be left free to execute the will of the people. I always have respected that will, and always shall.

Peace and universal prosperity, its sequence, with economy of administration, will lighten the burden of taxation, while it constantly reduces the national debt. Let us have peace.

46

The Democratic Party Platform
July 1868

At their National Convention, held in New York City, the Democratic party approved an election platform that largely consisted of opposition to Reconstruction and black suffrage. The presidential contest pitted former New York governor Horatio Seymour (Democrat) against Ulysses S. Grant (Republican). Grant won handily, thanks to the votes of southern African Americans enfranchised under the Reconstruction Act. In the northern states, however, the Democrats polled fairly well, suggesting the limits of northern patience with Republican Reconstruction. Though the Democratic platform must be recognized as overt partisan propaganda, its critique of congressional policy reflected significant popular opposition to the Reconstruction policies of the Republican party.

The Democratic party in National Convention assembled, reposing its trust in the intelligence, patriotism, and discriminating justice of the people, standing upon the Constitution as the foundation and limitation of the powers of the Government, and the guaranty of the liberties of the citizen, and recognizing the questions of Slavery and Secession as having been settled for all time to come by the war, or the voluntary action of the Southern States in constitutional conventions assembled, and never to be renewed or re-agitated, do with the return of peace demand:

From *The Democratic Speaker's Handbook* (Miami, Ohio: Miami Printing and Publishing Co., 1868), 224–26.

First. Immediate restoration of all the States to their rights in the Union, under the Constitution, and of Civil Government to the American people.

Second. Amnesty for all past political offenses and the regulation of the elective franchise in the States by their citizens. . . .

Sixth. Economy in the administration of the Government, the reduction of the standing army and navy, the abolition of the Freedmen's Bureau [great cheering] and all political instrumentalities designed to secure negro supremacy. . . .

Seventh. Reform of abuses in the Administration, the expulsion of corrupt men from office, the abrogation of useless offices, the restoration of rightful authority to and the independence of the Executive and Judicial Departments of the Government, the subordination of the military to the civil power, to the end that the usurpations of Congress and the despotism of the sword may cease. . . .

In demanding these measures and reforms we arraign the Radical party for its disregard of right and the unparalleled oppression and tyranny which have marked its career. After the most solemn and unanimous pledge of both Houses of Congress to prosecute the war exclusively for the maintenance of the Government and the preservation of the Union under the Constitution, it has repeatedly violated that most sacred pledge under which alone was rallied that noble volunteer army which carried our flag to victory. Instead of restoring the Union, it has, so far as in its power, dissolved it, and subjected ten States in time of profound peace to military despotism and negro supremacy. . . . It has stripped the President of his Constitutional power of appointment, even of his own Cabinet. Under its repeated assaults the pillars of the Government are rocking on their base, and should it succeed in November next and inaugurate its President, we will meet as a subject and conquered people amid the ruins of liberty and the shattered fragments of the Constitution; and we do declare and resolve, that ever since the people of the United States threw off all subjection to the British Crown the privilege and trust of suffrage have belonged to the several States, and have been granted, regulated, and controlled exclusively by the political power of each State respectively, and that any attempt by Congress, on any pretext whatever, to deprive any State of this right, or interfere with its exercise, is a flagrant usurpation of power which can find no warrant in the Constitution; and, if sanctioned by the people, will subvert our form of government, and can only end in a single centralized and consolidated government, in which the separate existence of the States will be entirely absorbed, and an unqualified despotism be established in place of a Federal Union of coequal States; and that we regard the Reconstruction acts (so called) of Congress, as such, usurpations and unconstitutional, revolutionary and void. . . .

That the President of the United States, Andrew Johnson [applause], in exercising the power of his high office in resisting the aggressions of Congress upon the constitutional rights of the States and the people, is entitled to the gratitude of the whole American people, and in behalf of the Democratic party we tender him our thanks for his patriotic efforts in that regard.

5

From Radicalism to Redemption

47

HENRY WILSON AND SAMUEL POMEROY

Speeches on the Fifteenth Amendment
January 28–29, 1869

By late 1868, Republicans had expanded the definition of citizenship and enshrined civil rights in the Constitution. They had provided southern freedpeople with the vote and set the course for the reintegration of a newly democratic South into the nation's body politic. But the revolution would go no further. Rather than pressing for additional reforms, congressional Republicans mainly sought to defend and support the body of legislation they had enacted in 1866 and 1867.

One final step remained, however. Although the southern state constitutions produced under the auspices of the Reconstruction Act guaranteed African American suffrage, congressional Republicans sought further security for black voting rights. In late 1868, they began debates on the Fifteenth Amendment. The amendment would provide African Americans outside the South with equal access to the ballot, while placing the right to vote on a more permanent, constitutional footing. Radical senators Henry Wilson (Massachusetts) and Samuel Pomeroy (Kansas) both spoke in favor of the amendment. Responding to Garrett Davis, Democratic senator from Kentucky, who had charged that Republicans were merely seeking to augment their vote totals through the enfranchisement of northern African Americans, Wilson insisted that his support of

From Cong. Globe, 40th Cong., 3d Sess., 672, 708.

the voting rights amendment was rooted in principle, not partisanship. Speaking the next day, Pomeroy gave an impassioned defense of equal rights that stands as a fitting capstone to a generation of Republican advocacy.

Mr. WILSON. . . . [T]he Senator from Kentucky tells us that in proposing this amendment we are seeking to perpetuate our power. A word to the Senator on that point. He knows and I know that this whole struggle in this country to give equal rights and equal privileges to all citizens of the United States has been an unpopular one; that we have been forced to struggle against passions and prejudices engendered by generations of wrong and oppression; that we have been compelled to struggle against great interests and powerful political organizations. I say to the Senator that the struggle of the last eight years to give freedom to four and a half millions of men who were held in slavery, to make them citizens of the United States, to clothe them with the right of suffrage, to give them the privilege to be voted for, to make them in all respects equal to the white citizens of the United States, has cost the party with which I act a quarter of a million of votes. There is not to-day a square mile in the United States where the advocacy of the equal rights and privileges of those colored men has not been in the past and is not now unpopular. Yes, sir, the cause of the poor, wronged, oppressed negroes has been, now is, and for some years will continue to be, an unpopular cause. The public man or the political party that honestly and zealously espouses their cause will continue to be misunderstood, misrepresented, and maligned. In the past the true and tried friend of the black man has been made to feel the hatred and power of the enemies of the black race. It is too much so now and I fear it will be so in some portions of the country for years to come.

But my doctrine is, no matter how unpopular it is, no matter what it costs, no matter whether it brings victory or defeat, it is our duty to hope on and struggle on and work on until we make the humblest citizen of the United States the peer and the equal in rights and privileges of every other citizen of the United States. Sir, I do not intend to cease in my efforts until that end is fully accomplished. Let us give to all citizens equal rights, and then protect everybody in the United States in the exercise of those rights. When we attain that position we shall have carried out logically the ideas that lie at the foundation of our institutions; we shall be in harmony with our professions; we shall have acted like a truly republican and Christian people. Until we do that we are in a false position, an illogical position — a position that cannot be defended;

a position that I believe is dishonorable to the nation with the lights we have before us. Through all the contests of the past thirty-five years I have looked to the final consummation of the perfect equality of citizens of the United States in rights and privileges and the complete protection of all citizens in their rights and privileges. Peace can only come in all its power and beauty by the complete triumph of equality and justice. . . .

Mr. POMEROY. Mr. President, during the discussion of this question yesterday the Senator from Massachusetts [Mr. WILSON] made use of the following words, as reported in the Globe:[1]

> "There is not to-day a square mile in the United States where the advocacy of the equal rights and privileges of those colored men has not been in the past and is not now unpopular."

And then he goes on to say that on every square mile the Republican party lost votes by its advanced views upon the question of equal rights. I only desire to reply to that in a word, as I did not have the opportunity then, that that is only one side-view of this question. Let it be known in this country that the Republican party have abandoned the cause of the rights of man, of the rights of the colored men of this country, and instead of losing a few thousand votes, as the Senator from Massachusetts intimated, I apprehend that the party itself would not be worth preserving. The strength of the Republican party consists in its adherence to principle, and to that embodiment of its principles, equality of rights among men. Without that, I repeat, there would be no motive to sustain the party, and the party would not be worth sustaining. It is, to my mind, all that makes it valuable. It was that for which it was organized; and instead of being a source of weakness it is, in my opinion, a source of strength and power.

---

[1] The *Congressional Globe* was the official record of Congress.

48

The Fifteenth Amendment to the U.S. Constitution
1870

The Fifteenth Amendment passed Congress on February 26, 1869. Three-quarters of the states had ratified the amendment by early 1870. In its final form, the amendment prevented the states and the federal government from denying the right to vote based on "race, color, or previous condition of servitude." During debates, more expansive proposals that outlawed the infringement of voting rights based on place of birth, property ownership, literacy, or religious beliefs were defeated. The final amendment also made no mention of discrimination on the basis of sex.

The failure to pass a more comprehensive voting rights amendment would have tragic consequences in the decades to come. By the 1890s, the southern states had begun to deploy a variety of means, including poll taxes and literacy tests, to prevent African Americans from voting. Even though such provisions violated the spirit (if not the letter) of the Fifteenth Amendment, the federal government did not intervene. Black suffrage—the central accomplishment of Radical Reconstruction—was all but nonexistent in the Jim Crow South. This state of affairs would persist until the civil rights movement and the passage of the Voting Rights Act of 1965.

SEC. 1. The right of citizens of the United States to vote shall not be denied or abridged by the United States or by any State on account of race, color, or previous condition of servitude.

SEC. 2. The Congress shall have power to enforce this article by appropriate legislation.

From Edward McPherson, *The Political History of the United States of America during the Period of Reconstruction* (Washington, D.C.: Philp & Solomons, 1871), 399.

49

FREDERICK DOUGLASS AND SUSAN B. ANTHONY
Debate Over Women's Suffrage
May 1869

At the May 1869 anniversary meeting of the American Equal Rights Association, the schism between women's suffrage reformers and defenders of African American rights was once again on prominent display. Although Frederick Douglass insisted that he was "in favor of women's suffrage," the black abolitionist argued that the physical violence to which African Americans were regularly subjected had made black suffrage a matter of life and death. In response, women's suffrage advocate Susan B. Anthony argued that the nation would have been wiser to enfranchise white women first. Women, Anthony argued, were better equipped to responsibly exercise the right to vote. The bitter exchange between former allies dramatized the possibilities and disappointments of the postwar moment. For all it accomplished, Radical Reconstruction failed to produce a truly universal suffrage.

Mr. DOUGLASS:—. . . I must say that I do not see how any one can pretend that there is the same urgency in giving the ballot to woman as to the negro. With us, the matter is a question of life and death, at least, in fifteen States of the Union. When women, because they are women, are hunted down through the cities of New York and New Orleans; when they are dragged from their houses and hung upon lamp-posts; when their children are torn from their arms, and their brains dashed out upon the pavement; when they are objects of insult and outrage at every turn; when they are in danger of having their homes burnt down over their heads; when their children are not allowed to enter schools; then they will have an urgency to obtain the ballot equal to our own. (Great applause.)

A VOICE:—Is that not all true about black women?

From Elizabeth Cady Stanton, Susan B. Anthony, and Matilda Joslyn Gage, eds., *History of Woman Suffrage* (Rochester, N.Y.: Charles Mann, 1887), 382–83.

Mr. DOUGLASS:—Yes, yes, yes; it is true of the black woman, but not because she is a woman, but because she is black. (Applause.) . . .

Miss ANTHONY:—The old anti-slavery school say women must stand back and wait until the negroes shall be recognized. But we say, if you will not give the whole loaf of suffrage to the entire people, give it to the most intelligent first. (Applause.) If intelligence, justice, and morality are to have precedence in the Government, let the question of woman be brought up first and that of the negro last. (Applause.) . . . When Mr. Douglass mentioned the black man first and the woman last, if he had noticed he would have seen that it was the men that clapped and not the women. There is not the woman born who desires to eat the bread of dependence, no matter whether it be from the hand of father, husband, or brother; for any one who does so eat her bread places herself in the power of the person from whom she takes it. (Applause.) Mr. Douglass talks about the wrongs of the negro; but with all the outrages that he to-day suffers, he would not exchange his sex and take the place of Elizabeth Cady Stanton.[1] (Laughter and applause.)

Mr. DOUGLASS:—I want to know if granting you the right of suffrage will change the nature of our sexes? (Great laughter.)

Miss ANTHONY:—It will change the pecuniary position of woman; it will place her where she can earn her own bread. (Loud applause.) She will not then be driven to such employments only as man chooses for her.

[1] Elizabeth Cady Stanton was another women's suffrage reformer. In his comments, Douglass had mentioned his longtime friendship with Stanton.

50

HIRAM R. REVELS

First Speech as a U.S. Senator

March 16, 1870

In February 1870, Hiram R. Revels became the first African American to serve as a U.S. senator. Revels was born free in North Carolina and educated in the Midwest. He moved to Mississippi after the Civil War. In 1870, the state's Republican-controlled legislature appointed him to fill a vacant Senate seat. Although he held the office for only a year, the selection of the nation's first black senator was an event of extraordinary symbolic significance. In his maiden speech, delivered during a debate over the readmission of Georgia, Revels offered a passionate defense of African American civil and political rights.

Mr. REVELS. Mr. President, I rise at this particular juncture in the discussion of the Georgia bill with feelings which perhaps never before entered into the experience of any member of this body. I rise, too, with misgivings as to the propriety of lifting my voice at this early period after my admission to the Senate. . . . When questions arise which bear upon the safety and protection of the loyal white and colored population of those States lately in rebellion I cannot allow any thought as to mere propriety to enter into my consideration of duty. The responsibilities of being the exponent of such a constituency as I have the honor to represent are fully appreciated by me. I bear about me daily the keenest sense of their weight, and that feeling prompts me now to lift my voice for the first time in this Council Chamber of the nation; and sir, I stand to-day on this floor to appeal for protection from the strong arm of the Government for her loyal children, irrespective of color and race, who are citizens of the southern States, and particularly the State of Georgia. . . .

Mr. President, I maintain that the past record of my race is a true index of the feelings which to-day animate them. They bear toward their former masters no revengeful thoughts, no hatreds, no animosities. They aim not to elevate themselves by sacrificing one single interest of

From Cong. Globe, 41st Cong., 2d Sess., 1986–88.

their white fellow-citizens. They ask but the rights which are theirs by God's universal law, and which are the natural outgrowth, the logical sequence of the condition in which the legislative enactments of this nation have placed them. They appeal to you and to me to see that they receive that protection which alone will enable them to pursue their daily avocations with success and enjoy the liberties of citizenship on the same footing with their white neighbors and friends. . . .

The Republican party is not inflamed, as some would fain have the country believe, against the white population of the South. Its borders are wide enough for all truly loyal men to find within them peace and repose from the din and discord of angry faction. And be that loyal man white or black, that great party of our Republic will, if consistent with the record it has already made for posterity, throw around him the same impartial security in his pursuit of liberty and happiness. . . .

Sir, I now leave this question to the consideration of this body, and I wish my last words upon the great issues involved in the bill before us to be my solemn and earnest demand for full and prompt protection for the helpless loyal people of Georgia.

51

CURRIER & IVES

The First Colored Senator and Representatives
1872

In 1872, the popular printmakers Currier & Ives produced this lithograph of the nation's first African American congressmen. Senator Hiram R. Revels is seated to the left. Joining him are Representatives Benjamin S. Turner (Alabama), Robert C. DeLarge (South Carolina), Josiah T. Walls (Florida), Jefferson F. Long (Georgia), Joseph H. Rainey (South Carolina), and Robert B. Elliott (South Carolina). All were members of the Republican party, and all represented states in the former Confederacy.

THE FIRST COLORED SENATOR AND REPRESENTATIVES.
In the 41ˢᵗ and 42ⁿᵈ Congress of the United States.

U.S. Senator H.R.REVELS. of Mississippi   BENJ. S.TURNER, M.C. of Alabama.   JOSIAH T. WALLS, M.C. of Florida.   JOSEPH H. RAINY, M.C. of S.Carolina.   R. BROWN ELLIOT, M.C. of S.Carolina.
    ROBERT C. DE LARGE, M.C. of S.Carolina.   JEFFERSON H. LONG, M.C. of Georgia.

139

52

ELIAS HILL

Testimony about a Ku Klux Klan Attack
1871

White-on-black racial violence had been a regular occurrence since the early days of Reconstruction (see Documents 15 and 22), but such violence escalated after the passage of the Reconstruction Act. The Ku Klux Klan was an organization of night-riding political terrorists devoted to the overthrow of black suffrage, the Republican party, and Reconstruction. Founded in Tennessee in 1866, the organization had spread across the South by 1868. The Klan routinely resorted to torture, rape, and murder in an attempt to keep black and white Republicans from voting, making speeches, or holding office.

In an attempt to control southern violence, the U.S. Congress passed a number of enforcement measures, culminating in the Ku Klux Klan Act of 1871. At the same time, Congress organized a committee to collect information on racial violence in the South. Senators and congressmen spread across the South, interviewing Klan members and Klan victims. In South Carolina, committee members spoke with Elias Hill, an African American minister. Hill, who had a serious physical disability, described a Ku Klux Klan attack in excruciating detail. His attackers demanded that Hill abandon the Republican party, suggesting the inextricable links between violence and politics in the Reconstruction South.

On the night of the 5th of last May, after I had heard a great deal of what they had done in that neighborhood, they came. It was between 12 and 1 o'clock at night, when I was awakened and heard the dogs barking, and something walking, very much like horses. As I had often laid awake listening for such persons, for they had been all through the neighborhood, and disturbed all men and many women, I supposed it was them. . . . One ran in the house, and stopping about the middle of the

From *Report of the Joint Select Committee to Inquire into the Condition of Affairs in the Late Insurrectionary States*, Vol. 5 (Washington, D.C.: Government Printing Office, 1872), 1406–8.

TESTIMONY ABOUT A KU KLUX KLAN ATTACK

house, which is a small cabin, he turned around as it seemed to me as I lay there, awake, and said "Who's here?" Then I knew they would take me, and I answered, "I am here." He shouted for joy, as it seemed, "Here he is! Here he is! We have found him!" and he threw the bed-clothes off of me and caught me by one arm, while another man took me by the other and they carried me into the yard between the houses. . . . They pointed pistols at me all around my head once or twice, as if they were going to shoot me, telling me they were going to kill me, wasn't I ready to die? and willing to die? didn't I preach? that they came to kill me — all the time pointing pistols at me. . . . One caught me by the leg and hurt me, for my leg for forty years has been drawn each year, more and more year by year, and I made moan when it hurt so. One said "G–d d——n it, hush!" He had a horsewhip, and he told me to pull up my shirt and he hit me. He told me at every lick "Hold up your shirt." I made a moan every time he cut me with the horsewhip. I reckon he struck me eight cuts right on the hip bone. . . . They all had disguises on. . . . One of them took a strap and buckled it around my neck and said, "Let's take him to the river and drown him." . . . They said "Look here! Will you put a card in the paper next week like June Moore and Sol Hill?["] They had been prevailed on to put a card in the paper to renounce all republicanism and never vote. . . . They asked me, "Will you quit preaching?" I told them I did not know. I said that to save my life. They said I must stop that republican paper that was coming to Clay Hill. . . . The republican weekly paper was then coming to me from Charleston. It came to my name. They said I must stop it, quit preaching, and put a card in the newspaper renouncing republicanism, and they would not kill me; but if I did not they would come back the next week and kill me.

53

"Veni Vidi" Describes the Violence of Redemption in Mississippi

July 1875

---

*While federal action had effectively quashed the Ku Klux Klan by
1872, racial violence remained a central part of southern politics for
the remainder of Reconstruction. A variety of white terrorist organizations — including the White League and the Red Shirts — picked up where
the Ku Klux Klan left off, terrorizing black Republicans across the South.
In 1875, an African American paper published in Philadelphia printed
a description of racial violence in Vicksburg, Mississippi. The correspondent, using the name* Veni Vidi *(Latin for "I came, I saw"), described
a white mob's attack on a peaceful Independence Day celebration. The
attack was part of a coordinated effort to restore white Democratic
control in Mississippi, a process popularly known as "Redemption." The
violence served its intended purpose; the state returned to Democratic
hands following the 1875 elections.*

Mr. EDITOR: — Allow me space in your paper to lay before your readers,
and I trust through that medium, the whole American people, one of
the most outrageous and sickening affairs it has ever been my lot to witness, even in this blood-thirsty section of our country.

About ten days ago a few respectable colored men in conversation
concerning the centennial celebration going on throughout the country
and the general feeling of amity and fraternity which seemed to be setting in on all sides, both south and north, suggested the idea of a small
celebration here on Independence day. . . . Accordingly, on Monday,
July 5th, two or three hundred people, mostly colored, came in from the
surrounding country. . . . The meeting organized and the proceeding
opened with the reading of the Declaration of Independence by one of
the colored ministers of the city. After reading was concluded a patriotic air was played by the band in attendance, and then Judge Brown[1]

---

[1] George F. Brown, a white Republican circuit court judge.

From "Another Chapter of Blood at Vicksburg," *The Christian Recorder*, 22 July 1875, 1.

addressed the assembly in a calm, deliberate manner. . . . His speech was entirely free from any thing offensive whatever to the people of either class or section of the country. He was followed by secretary of State Hill (colored),[2] whose remarks though not ultra or [acrimonious], were nevertheless not so guarded and discreet as we thought they ought to have been. When he had been speaking about twenty minutes, a file of white men were noticed coming into the room, and immediately arranged themselves in regular file along one side of the house. Within five minutes a scuffle began at the head of their line on the left of the crowd, and then a pistol shot followed, whereupon the whole line presented revolvers and ordered the meeting to disperse. The colored people as usual took panic and made one grand rush for the door. Of course they could not all pass through the door, and a rush was made for the windows, which are twenty or twenty-five feet above ground. The mob began to beat and pound with their revolvers the straggling few that remained behind. . . .

The colored people lingered about the campus for some time, when a pistol shot gave the signal, and those fearful Winchester rifles were turned upon the defenseless mass of colored humanity. I suppose as many as one hundred shots were fired in the space of two minutes. Two men were killed and a number wounded; some of whom have since died. . . .

Thus ended the ninety ninth anniversary of American freedom (?) and independence in a free (?) American city. It is a crime unto death to meet and read the declaration of human freedom. . . .

Cry peace, peace, there is no peace. . . . Forsaken by their late northern friends, that is, friends and even brothers so long as they needed help, persecuted by their old masters whom they are utterly unable to withstand—wretched indeed will the condition of the black man soon be in these states.

Veni Vidi.

---

[2] James Hill served as Mississippi's secretary of state from 1874 to 1878.

54

RUTHERFORD B. HAYES

Inaugural Address

March 5, 1877

By 1876, it was clear that the northern public had lost much of its appetite for the "southern question." The Republican party's 1876 platform did not have much to say about Reconstruction, nor did the party's presidential candidate, Ohio governor Rutherford B. Hayes. In an extraordinarily close and deeply controversial election, Hayes defeated the Democratic candidate, Samuel J. Tilden. At the same time, the victories of Democratic candidates for governor in Louisiana, South Carolina, and Florida—the only southern states that had remained in Republican control prior to the election—completed the "Redemption" of the former Confederacy. Hayes's inaugural address was noteworthy for its conciliatory tone toward the white South. As president, Hayes sought to foster reunion between the sections. He turned away from the sort of interventionism that had marked Grant's second term, allowing southerners to manage their own political affairs largely free of federal oversight. While quite popular among many northern Republicans, this policy would have negative ramifications for southern Republicanism and for African American civil and political rights.

The permanent pacification of the country upon such principles and by such measures as will secure the complete protection of its citizens in the free enjoyment of their constitutional rights is now the one subject, in our public affairs, which all thoughtful and patriotic citizens regard as of supreme importance. . . .

The sweeping revolution of the entire labor system of a large portion of our country, and the advance of four millions of people from a condition of servitude to that of citizenship, upon an equal footing with their former masters, could not occur without presenting problems of the gravest moment, to be dealt with by the emancipated race, by their

From *Letters and Messages of Rutherford B. Hayes, President of the United States, Together with Letter of Acceptance and Inaugural Address* (Washington, D.C.: n.p., 1881), 11–13.

former masters, and by the General Government, the author of the act of emancipation. That it was a wise, just, and Providential act, fraught with good for all concerned, is now generally conceded throughout the country. That a moral obligation rests upon the National Government to employ its constitutional power and influence to establish the rights of the people it has emancipated, and to protect them in the enjoyment of those rights when they are infringed or assailed, is also generally admitted.

The evils which afflict the Southern States can only be removed or remedied by the united and harmonious efforts of both races, actuated by motives of mutual sympathy and regard. And while in duty bound and fully determined to protect the rights of all by every constitutional means at the disposal of my administration, I am sincerely anxious to use every legitimate influence in favor of honest and efficient local self-government as the true resource of those States for the promotion of the contentment and prosperity of their citizens. In the effort I shall make to accomplish this purpose I ask the cordial co-operation of all who cherish an interest in the welfare of the country, trusting that party ties and the prejudice of race will be freely surrendered in behalf of the great purpose to be accomplished. . . .

Let me assure my countrymen of the Southern States that it is my earnest desire to regard and promote their truest interests, the interests of the white and of the colored people both, and equally, and to put forth my best efforts in behalf of a civil policy which will forever wipe out in our political affairs the color line, and the distinction between North and South, to the end that we may have not merely a united North or a united South, but a united country.

A Chronology of Radical Reconstruction (1863–1877)

1863 *January 1* President Abraham Lincoln signs the Emancipation Proclamation.

December 8 In his Proclamation of Amnesty, Lincoln lays out his Ten Percent Plan for Reconstruction.

1864 *July* Passage of the Wade-Davis Bill, containing the congressional plan for Reconstruction. Lincoln pocket vetoes the bill. Benjamin Wade and Henry Winter Davis write the Wade-Davis Manifesto.

1865 *January 31* Congress approves the Thirteenth Amendment.

April 14–15 President Lincoln assassinated; Andrew Johnson becomes president.

May 29 In his "May Proclamations," Andrew Johnson sets the course for Presidential Reconstruction.

Summer–Fall Southern states call conventions to redraft their constitutions under Andrew Johnson's authority. State legislatures reconvene and pass "Black Codes." Southern states select senators and representatives.

December 4 Congress comes back into session (39th Congress, 1st Session). House and Senate refuse to seat southern claimants.

December 6 States ratify the Thirteenth Amendment.

1866 *March 13* Congress passes the Civil Rights Bill.

March 27 Andrew Johnson vetoes the Civil Rights Bill.

April 9 Congress overrides Johnson's veto of the Civil Rights Bill.

May 1–3 Memphis riot.

June 13 Congress approves the Fourteenth Amendment.

Fall–Winter Southern state legislatures fail to ratify the Fourteenth Amendment.

November   Republican candidates sweep to victory in midterm congressional elections. Republicans secure veto-proof majority in the next session of Congress.

1867   *March 2*   Congress passes the Reconstruction Act over Johnson's veto. Congress passes the Tenure of Office Act over Johnson's veto.

August 12   With Senate out of session, Andrew Johnson suspends Secretary of War Edwin Stanton.

Fall–Winter   Following the procedure laid out in the Reconstruction Act, conventions meet to redraft southern state constitutions. African Americans are eligible to vote for and serve as delegates.

1868   *January 13*   Senate refuses to uphold the suspension of Secretary of War Stanton.

February 21   Andrew Johnson replaces Stanton with General Lorenzo Thomas, in violation of the Tenure of Office Act.

February 24   House of Representatives approves impeachment resolution.

March 30   Impeachment trial begins in the Senate.

May 16   Senate fails to convict Johnson on eleventh article of impeachment.

May 26   Senate fails to convict Johnson on second and third articles of impeachment, ending the trial.

July 9   States ratify the Fourteenth Amendment.

November 3   Republican Ulysses S. Grant elected president.

1869   *February 26*   Congress approves the Fifteenth Amendment.

1870   *February 3*   States ratify the Fifteenth Amendment.

February 25   Hiram Revels of Mississippi becomes the first African American to serve in the U.S. Senate.

1871   *April 20*   Congress passes the Ku Klux Klan Act, allowing President Grant to take steps to suppress southern racial violence.

1872   *November 5*   Grant reelected president.

1877   *March 5*   Republican Rutherford B. Hayes is inaugurated as president. Controversial election also sees the return of Florida, South Carolina, and Louisiana to Democratic control, completing the Redemption of the South.

Questions for Consideration

1. What were the major challenges facing policymakers in the aftermath of the Civil War?
2. How did wartime debates over Reconstruction anticipate the political struggles of the early postwar era?
3. What was the political worldview of the Radical Republicans?
4. What was Andrew Johnson's political ideology, and why did he disagree with the Radical Republicans?
5. How did the actions of the white South shape Reconstruction policy between 1865 and 1867?
6. What role did the "grasp of war" doctrine play in formulating and justifying congressional Reconstruction policy?
7. Is the Fourteenth Amendment best understood as a Radical document or a moderate one? Why?
8. Why had congressional Republicans come to consider black suffrage essential to the Reconstruction of the South by 1867?
9. What was the chain of events leading to the passage of the Reconstruction Act of 1867?
10. Why did some Radicals support the redistribution of land? Why did moderates and conservative Republicans oppose it? How would the implementation of this policy have affected the subsequent history of Reconstruction?
11. Were the impeachment proceedings against Andrew Johnson justified? Why or why not?
12. What effect did Radical Reconstruction have on the lives of southern African Americans? On southern whites?
13. Why did women's rights advocates object to parts of the congressional Reconstruction program?
14. How did Reconstruction alter the meaning of American citizenship?

15. How did Reconstruction change the relationship between Americans and the federal government? Between the states and the federal government?

16. What was the role of violence in the Redemption of the South?

17. Why did Radical Reconstruction ultimately fail to protect the civil and political rights of southern African Americans?

18. How radical was Radical Reconstruction?

Selected Bibliography

OVERVIEWS OF RECONSTRUCTION

Egerton, Douglas R. *The Wars of Reconstruction: The Brief, Violent History of America's Most Progressive Era.* New York: Bloomsbury Press, 2014.

Fitzgerald, Michael W. *Splendid Failure: Postwar Reconstruction in the American South.* Chicago: Ivan R. Dee, 2007.

Foner, Eric. *Reconstruction: America's Unfinished Revolution, 1863–1877.* New York: Harper & Row, 1988.

Franklin, John Hope. *Reconstruction after the Civil War.* 1961. Reprint, Chicago: University of Chicago Press, 1994.

Perman, Michael. *Reunion without Compromise: The South and Reconstruction, 1865–1868.* New York: Cambridge University Press, 1973.

Simpson, Brooks D. *The Reconstruction Presidents.* Lawrence: University Press of Kansas, 1998.

Summers, Mark Wahlgren. *The Ordeal of the Reunion: A New History of Reconstruction.* Chapel Hill: University of North Carolina Press, 2014.

RADICAL RECONSTRUCTION

Benedict, Michael Les. *A Compromise of Principle: Congressional Republicans and Reconstruction, 1863–1869.* New York: W. W. Norton & Company, 1974.

———. *The Impeachment and Trial of Andrew Johnson.* New York: W. W. Norton & Company, 1973.

Donald, David. *Charles Sumner and the Rights of Man.* New York: Random House, 1970.

Dray, Philip. *Capitol Men: The Epic Story of Reconstruction through the Lives of the First Black Congressmen.* New York: Mariner Books, 2010.

Epps, Garrett. *Democracy Reborn: The Fourteenth Amendment and the Fight for Equal Rights in Post–Civil War America.* New York: Henry Holt, 2006.

Gillette, William. *The Right to Vote: Politics and the Passage of the 15th Amendment.* Baltimore, Md.: Johns Hopkins University Press, 1969.

McKitrick, Eric L. *Andrew Johnson and Reconstruction.* New York: Oxford University Press, 1960.

Trefousse, Hans L. *The Radical Republicans: Lincoln's Vanguard for Racial Justice*. New York: Alfred A. Knopf, 1969.
————. *Thaddeus Stevens: Nineteenth-Century Egalitarian*. Chapel Hill: University of North Carolina Press, 1997.
Vorenberg, Michael. *Final Freedom: The Civil War, the Abolition of Slavery, and the Thirteenth Amendment*. New York: Cambridge University Press, 2004.

RACE AND RECONSTRUCTION IN THE SOUTH

Blight, David. *Race and Reunion: The Civil War in American Memory*. Cambridge, Mass.: Harvard University Press, 2001.
Downs, Gregory P. *Declarations of Dependence: The Long Reconstruction of Popular Politics in the South, 1861–1908*. Chapel Hill: University of North Carolina Press, 2011.
Edwards, Laura F. *Gendered Strife and Confusion: The Political Culture of Reconstruction*. Urbana: University of Illinois Press, 1997.
Emberton, Carole. *Beyond Redemption: Race, Violence, and the American South after the Civil War*. Chicago: University of Chicago Press, 2013.
Hahn, Steven. *A Nation under Our Feet: Black Political Struggles in the Rural South from Slavery to the Great Migration*. Cambridge, Mass.: Harvard University Press, 2005.
Hunter, Tera W. *To 'Joy My Freedom: Southern Black Women's Lives and Labors after the Civil War*. Cambridge, Mass.: Harvard University Press, 1998.
Litwack, Leon. *Been in the Storm So Long: The Aftermath of Slavery*. New York: Alfred A. Knopf, 1979.
Masur, Kate. *An Example for All the Land: Emancipation and the Struggle over Equality in Washington, D.C.* Chapel Hill: University of North Carolina Press, 2010.
O'Donovan, Susan Eva. *Becoming Free in the Cotton South*. Cambridge, Mass.: Harvard University Press, 2007.
Ortiz, Paul. *Emancipation Betrayed: The Hidden History of Black Organizing and White Violence in Florida from Reconstruction to the Bloody Election of 1920*. Berkeley: University of California Press, 2006.
Rodrigue, John C. *Reconstruction in the Cane Fields: From Slavery to Free Labor in Louisiana's Sugar Parishes, 1862–1880*. Baton Rouge: Louisiana State University Press, 2001.
Rosen, Hannah. *Terror in the Heart of Freedom: Citizenship, Sexual Violence, and the Meaning of Race in the Postemancipation South*. Chapel Hill: University of North Carolina Press, 2009.
Saville, Julie. *The Work of Reconstruction: From Slave to Wage Laborer in South Carolina, 1860–1870*. New York: Cambridge University Press, 1994.

Index

153

U.S. House of Representatives
African Americans serving in, 21
articles of impeachment against Johnson, 121–23
House Judiciary Committee report on impeachment, 117
impeachment vote, 124–25
U.S. Senate
African Americans serving in, 21
first African American in, 137–38

Vagrant Act, Mississippi, 57–58
"Veni Vidi" Describes the Violence of Redemption in Mississippi, 142–43
Veto of the Civil Rights Bill (Johnson), 74–76
veto power, 37, 118–19
Vicksburg, Mississippi, 142–43
Virginia, 33, 91
voting rights. *See also* African American suffrage
of African Americans, 3, 6, 8, 21, 111–12
Civil Rights Bill and, 73
Constitution and, 16, 44, 60, 102
Fifteenth Amendment and, 24, 134
Fourteenth Amendment and, 16
of freedmen, 109
Radical Republicans and, 6
subversion of, 134
of white southerners, 10–11
of women, 17, 60–61, 135–36
Voting Rights Act of 1965, 134

Wade, Benjamin, 7, 10–11, 23, 90, 124, 147
abolitionism and, 4
Speech on the "Great Principle of Eternal Justice," 67–69
Wade-Davis Manifesto, 37–39
Wade-Davis Bill/Manifesto, 10–11, 147
Lincoln's pocket veto of, 37
text of, 37–39
Walls, Josiah T., 138, 139*f*
Ward, Hamilton, 102
Speech on Radical Republicanism, 99–101

wartime Reconstruction, 9–11
Waud, A. R., *"The First Vote,"* 111, 112*f*
White League, 25, 142
white southerners. *See also* Confederate states (former)
African American attitudes toward, 137–38
attitudes of, 65–67
discrimination against, 75–76, 129–30
emancipation and, 144–45
Fourteenth Amendment and, 17
Hayes and, 144–45
Johnson and, 13, 116
land redistribution and, 6
landed aristocracy, 12, 108
loyalty oaths required from, 10
northern sympathy for, 1
racial violence and, 142–43
Radical Reconstruction and, 9
Report of the Joint Select Committee on Reconstruction, 80–82
Republican party and, 138
voting rights for, 10–11
white supremacists
impact of, 27–28
Jim Crow system and, 24, 26
Johnson as, 12, 15
Memphis, Tennessee, massacre and, 78–79
Wilson, Henry, 5
Speeches on the Fifteenth Amendment, 131–33
Wirz, Henry, 48*n*2
Wisconsin, 55
women
African American, 126, 135–36
economic status of, 136
Fourteenth Amendment and, 85
voting rights for, 17, 60–61, 85, 135–36
women's rights movement, 60–61
women's suffrage
debate over, 135–36
Stanton and, 60–61

Advisory Editors: Lynn Hunt, David W. Blight, and Bonnie G. Smith

Praise for Radical Reconstruction

"This volume is an invaluable guide to the tangled history of Reconstruction, the development of the first civil rights movement in America, and the often inspiring story of a group of politicians who helped usher in a new era of race relations in politics, law, and society."

—Joan Waugh, *University of California, Los Angeles*

"This is a first-rate and very readable documentary overview of Radical Reconstruction that does not lose its undergraduate readers in a sea of details."

—Alan Downs, *Georgia Southern University*

"This book will help students (and teachers) think *better* about this important and often confusing period."

—Kate Masur, *Northwestern University*

About the author

D, Yale University) is Assistant Professor
rsity of South Florida, where he
y of the nineteenth and twentieth
with an emphasis on the culture, society,
South. He is the author of *Stories of the*
of Southern Identity, 1865-1915, and
h study of Robert Charles and the New

DANIEL M. DEUTSCHLANDER

Civil Government

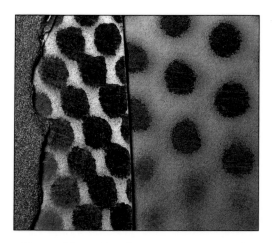

God's Other Kingdom

People's
B**I**BLE
Teachings